# Preparing
## *for the*
# SECOND COMING

TALKS AND FIRESIDES BY ERIC D. RICHARDS:

*Don't Look Back: You're Not Going That Way!*

*Change Your Words, Change Your World*

*Are You a Bushel or a Candlestick?*

# PREPARING
## *for the*
# SECOND
# COMING

# ERIC D. RICHARDS

Covenant Communications, Inc.

Cover image: *Diwali Oil Lamp* © phive2015, courtesy istockphoto.com.

Cover design copyright © 2017 by Covenant Communications, Inc.

Published by Covenant Communications, Inc.
American Fork, Utah

Printed in the United States of America
First Printing: August 2017

23 22 21 20 19 18 17   10 9 8 7 6 5 4 3 2 1

ISBN 978-1-52440-353-9

# Table of Contents

*Preface and Forewords*

*Blessed is he that* readeth*, and they that* hear *the words of this prophecy, and*
keep those things *which are written therein: for the time is at hand.*
                                              Revelation 1:3, emphases added

*[B]lessed is he that* keepeth *the sayings of the prophecy of this book.*
                                              Revelation 22:7, emphasis added

THESE PASSAGES FROM THE BOOK of Revelation have inspired me to create
this book of principles relevant for personal application in preparing
for the Second Coming of Jesus Christ. In addition to learning about
the apocalyptic events seen by John and with my emphasis on personal,
relevant application in mind, I invite you to *read* the book of Revelation,
*hear* the messages regarding the signs of the times, and *keep* or apply the
principles delineated.

A good friend of mine, Terry White, sat down with me many years ago
and together we began composing an outline of John's prophetic vision.
Ever since then, my personal study of John the Revelator's record has been
an absolute delight.

The Prophet Joseph Smith said, "The book of Revelation is one of
the plainest books God ever caused to be written,"[1] and President Marion
G. Romney taught, "Not only do I hope that we are familiar with these
coming events; I hope also that we keep the vision of them continually
before our minds . . . because upon a knowledge of them, and an
assurance of their reality . . . rests the efficacy of Christ's admonition, 'be
not troubled' (D&C 45:35)."[2] I hope this work provides a few insights

---

1 *History of the Church*, vol 5, 342.
2 Marion G. Romney, "Be Not Troubled," *Conference Report*, Oct. 1966, 50–54.

and several personal applications from the book of Revelation to bless your life and leave you at peace as you prepare for the Savior's return.

**FOREWORDS**

Brother Richards is an outstanding gospel teacher, and his work in this book can help us all become better gospel learners. The book of Revelation opens itself to many different interpretations, and Brother Richards has given us a wonderful starting point in our own study. This book, with insights from modern prophets and application questions throughout, brings the scriptures to life and invites the personal reflection in which we all must engage as we prepare to greet the Lord.

    —Brad Wilcox, BYU professor and author of *The Continuous Atonement* and *Changed through His Grace*

Eric is a master teacher! In this book, the book of Revelation is brought to life. Youth and adults of all ages can become engaged in understanding the events of the Second Coming and the prophecies in the book of Revelation, and they will be inspired to prepare themselves for this, the great event of our Savior's return.

    —Hank Smith, Popular Latter-day Saint speaker and author of *Be Happy: Simple Secrets to a Happier Life* and *Mothers Are Like . . .*

*Introduction*

A SEVEN-HEADED BEAST? FOUR BEASTS with six wings? A man eating a bitter little book that was as sweet as honey? Twenty-four elders and 144,000 servants? A great red dragon and a woman in the wilderness? The number 666? The book of Revelation can be captivating, if not a bit bewildering. Yet a careful look at the interpretations and applications of these symbols and prophecies is one key to preparing for the Second Coming and enjoying a study of John's panoramic vision. Elder Bruce R. McConkie said,

> Are we expected to understand the book of Revelation? Certainly. Why else did the Lord reveal it? The common notion that it deals with beasts and plagues and mysterious symbolisms that cannot be understood is just not true. . . . [I]f we apply ourselves with full purpose of heart, we can catch the vision of what the ancient Revelator recorded.[3]

A key to successful study of Revelation (or any book of scripture) is to mine and extract principles from the scriptural text. Elder Richard G. Scott taught:

> As you seek spiritual knowledge, search for principles. Carefully separate them from the detail used to explain them. Principles are concentrated truth, packaged for application to a wide variety of circumstances. . . . It is worth great effort to organize the truth we gather to simple statements of principle.[4]

3 Bruce R. McConkie, "Understanding the Book of Revelation," *Ensign,* Sept. 1975.
4 Richard G. Scott, "Acquiring Spiritual Knowledge," *Ensign,* Nov. 1993.

President Boyd K. Packer similarly taught:

> A principle is an enduring truth, a law, a rule you can adopt to guide you in making decisions. Generally principles are not spelled out in detail. That leaves you free to find your way with an enduring truth, a principle, as your anchor.[5]

President Russell M. Nelson counseled that when reading the scriptures we should pause and ask questions such as, "What principle can be learned from these teachings of the Lord?"[6] In addition, questions like, *What can I learn from this situation?* or, *What is the author of this passage trying to teach?* often highlight hidden principles for application and self-evaluation.

Discovering doctrines and finding relevant principles for application is comparable to panning for gold. Gold can be found among the rocks and gravel of riverbeds across the world, but oftentimes, the exposure of a gold nugget requires rock to be mined and processed. Like gold nuggets, some principles and doctrines are easy to spot, while others require a bit more mining.

To use another analogy, think of different news sources. We can tune in and watch or listen to world, national, state, and even local news specific to our community. If we were seeking information about a city council meeting, we wouldn't tune into a world or national news source; we would usually seek out our local news sources online, via TV, or a local newspaper because we are after specific information that is relevant to our circumstance. This book will give the overview of each chapter in Revelation (the *world news*) and then walk through the process of applying the message personally to our life through the Holy Ghost (tuning into the *local news*), ensuring that our application is consistent with revealed doctrine and principles.[7]

To help excavate golden principles for application as you study scripture, you might ask the following three questions along the way:

1. What principles is the Lord presenting through these words or symbols?
2. In what ways have I seen these principles manifested in real life?

5 Boyd K. Packer, "The Word of Wisdom: The Principle and the Promises," *Ensign*, May 1996.
6 Russell M. Nelson, "Living by Scriptural Guidance," *Ensign*, Nov. 2000.
7 This process is very helpful when reading the scriptures or while studying the gospel in general.

3.  What relevance do these principles have in my current life, and how can I apply them now?

The prophecies, events, inspired words, and stories within the book of Revelation (and in any scripture) are laden with doctrines and principles for application. If readers are fixed primarily upon the black words on the white pages, treasures will be overlooked. As President Marion G. Romney stated, "The scriptures have been written to preserve principles."[8] The quotes and statements that are presented in this book and that help provide ideas for application are primarily taken from statements made by latter-day prophets and Apostles, to help understand context and doctrine; a few statements made by other General Authorities have been included as well. These are shared to give background to some prophecies about the Second Coming and the meaning of some of the great symbols in Revelation.

As a rule of thumb, following is the hierarchy of where to turn for pure doctrines:[9]

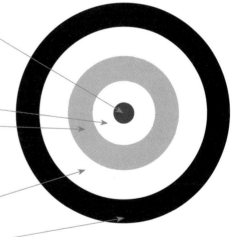

1. OFFICIAL PRONOUNCEMENTS OF THE FIRST PRESIDENCY
The current prophet's statements (usually in conjunction with his counselors) on doctrine, policy, etc.; usually given in general conferences, official correspondence, and/or through media

2. THE STANDARD WORKS
The four approved canonized scriptures

3. WRITINGS APPROVED BY THE CHURCH
Publications used with Church sanction in priesthood and auxiliary classes (e.g., *Jesus the Christ, A Marvelous Work and A Wonder, Articles of Faith, Priesthood and Church Government, Our Heritage, True to the Faith*, conference reports, Church manuals and magazines, *Our Search for Happiness*)

4. PERSONAL WRITINGS OF GENERAL AUTHORITIES
General Authorities' writings not on the same level as number three (e.g., *Mormon Doctrine, Man: His Origin and Destiny, Gospel Ideals, Doctrines of Salvation, The Miracle of Forgiveness*)

5. OTHER CHURCH WRITINGS
The written works of other Church members

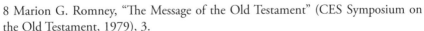

8 Marion G. Romney, "The Message of the Old Testament" (CES Symposium on the Old Testament, 1979), 3.

9 Sunday School handout based on Lowell L. Bennion's Book, *Religion and the Pursuit of Truth* (Salt Lake City: Deseret Book, 1968), 141–150. Note that because they are given in our day, prounouncements from the current First Presidency are of even greater emphasis for study than the Standard Works, which are of almost as great importance (ancient prophets also saw and prophesied of things relevant and pertaining to our day).

I also highly recommend studying these six resources to learn more about the events surrounding Christ's return:

- "Book of Revelation Overview" (*Ensign*, Oct. 1983).
- Gerald N. Lund, "Seeing the Book of Revelation As a Book of Revelation" (*Ensign*, Dec. 1987).
- *New Testament Student Manual* (IRI, 2014).
- *New Testament: Study Guide for Home-Study Seminary Students* (IRI, 2016).
- *Jesus Christ and the Everlasting Gospel Student Readings* (2016).
- *Gospel Principles* (IRI, 2011).

**THE PATTERN OF THIS BOOK**

In this book, I will first provide some commentary on the context of the chapter (it will be helpful if you read the verses mentioned and ideally the entire chapter in conjunction). Following this, I will present possible applications of principles taught in the passage. Finally, each block of scripture commentary will conclude in a section titled *Application*, with a relevant question for personal application for readers to consider.[10]

For instance, if this introduction were written about the first chapter of Revelation, you would read about John being banished to the Isle of Patmos, located off the west coast of what is now Turkey; while there, he used his time of captivity to receive revelation, which provides at least one principle for application: the wise use of time, both during adversity as well as in peaceful periods of life.

Paul, while imprisoned, wrote his best letters. Joseph Smith received some of the greatest revelations while in Liberty Jail. The prophet Moroni shared amazing insights as he wandered in the wilderness. From David to Abraham to Moses and Joseph, from Deborah to Mary, the list of great men and women of God who did some of their greatest work during times of captivity goes on and on. Even during times of adversity, we too can learn to use our time well.

Elder Dallin H. Oaks is a great example of the effective use of time. For instance, "[H]e takes seriously the scriptural admonition to 'cease to sleep longer than is needful' (D&C 88:124). What's needful for him is about six and a half hours—so that's what he takes, 'six if [he needs] more working time, seven if [he's] trying to catch up on lost sleep."[11]

---

10 For further study, a list of single-sentence sermons and information about the symbolism of numbers as used in the scriptures is provided in the Appendix.
11 Lavina Anderson, "Dallin H. Oaks: The Disciplined Edge," *Ensign*, Apr. 1981.

> [Elder Oaks's motto is,] "Work first, play later." His family, though, says they are tempted to change it to: "Work first, play never." Elder Oaks is good natured about it. He says what it means is that he rarely does something *only* to have fun, but rather that "I just have fun at [whatever] I do."[12]

He is a great example of finding positive things to do during discretionary times of life. As Psalms 90:12 counsels, "So teach us to number our days, that we may apply our hearts unto wisdom." If we can take count of our days, hours, and minutes and find ways to improve our time, we will gain wisdom and bless others in the process, which is something that John certainly did while on Patmos.

James, the brother of Jesus, wrote, "For what is your life? It is even a vapour, that appeareth for a little time, and then vanisheth away" (James 4:14). Our lives will be over in an instant, so we must ever be on the lookout for ways to improve our use of time. Because of technology, most of us have far more discretionary time than our ancestors. The Lord has counseled, "Thou shalt not idle away thy time" (D&C 60:13) and, "Cease to be idle" (D&C 88:124). We certainly don't want to be *too busy*, and we should remember the wise counsel and comforting assurance of King Benjamin, who taught, "[I]t is not requisite that a man should run faster than he has strength" (Mosiah 4:27), but we should examine our lives and see if there's something better we could be doing during our *in-between* moments of the day.

## AN APPLICATION

*How are you spending your discretionary time? Is there something you could be doing in those quiet moments that will strengthen your relationship with other people or with your Savior Jesus Christ?*

I would like to offer three cautions as you read this book. First, please know that it is challenging to know John's true intent as he was writing the 404 verses[13] in the book of Revelation. Because of this, some of the applications that I have drawn in this study might be stretching John's original intent. As we look at the doctrines presented by John and latter-day commentaries that help to clarify, you will learn to make relevant and personal application that points *you* to Christ. After all, He is the mark we are all looking to (see Jacob 4:4).

---

12 "Elder Dallin H. Oaks," *The Church of Jesus Christ of Latter-day Saints*, lds.org/prophets-and-apostles/, accessed Jun. 25, 2017.

13 This book will cover almost 300 of the verses (nearly 75 percent) of Revelation.

Second, please know that the fulfillment of these events is rather nebulous. Yes, some prophets and Apostles and Christian theologians have interpreted many of the events in Revelation, but the timing, sequence, and meaning of some events prophesied by John are unclear. When you and I greet each other in heaven (assuming we both wind up there), we might both grab a copy of this book (assuming, of course, this book makes it to heaven too!) and have a fantastic conversation with each other as we look at how the events really did play out.

And now, a final caution. Oftentimes when we study and make applications, we tend to get a bit overwhelmed or discouraged. As we read and mark and make lists of things we should be doing better, it can become disheartening that there's so much we need to improve upon. Sometimes it feels like we are being buried. Please know this: there is a difference between being buried and being planted. This book is meant to help you become *planted* in the gospel and not *buried* within it. The difference between being *planted* and being *buried* boils down to the expectation of what happens next. When you put a seed in the ground, you don't think to yourself, *I'm burying this seed.* You think, *I'm planting this seed.* You see, when you plant a seed, you expect to see it rise again and come to life. By way of application, when you go through tough times or when you feel overwhelmed by a celestial checklist, you may feel like you are being buried, but the fact is, it might simply be that you are being planted. Being planted means you're coming back—and not only that, but you are coming back better, increased, and stronger! You go in as a seed, but because of the life and spirit of God, you come out growing and blossoming, and you ultimately produce a beautiful harvest.

Please keep the words of President Gordon B. Hinckley close to your heart and mind. He simply said, "[T]ry a little harder to be a little better."[14] To further amplify this message, Elder David A. Bednar similarly taught, "If today you are a little bit better than you were yesterday, then that's enough. And, if tomorrow you are a little bit better than you were today, then that's enough."[15]

## BACKGROUND TO THE BOOK OF REVELATION

First of all, John's book is called *The Revelation of St. John the Divine.* Readers and scholars simply refer to it as *the book of Revelation.* Note that the word Revelation in the book's title is singular. Many people

14 Gordon B. Hinckley, "We have a Work to Do," *Ensign*, May 1995.
15 David A. Bednar, *Act in Doctrine: Spiritual Patterns for Turning from Self to the Savior* (Salt Lake City: Deseret Book, 2012).

erroneously call it *Revelations*. The title of the book in Greek is *Apocalypsis*, which is formed from two Greek words—*apo,* a preposition denoting *separation* or *removal;* and *kalypto,* a verb meaning to *cover, hide,* or *veil. Revelation,* then, literally means *removal of the veil or covering.*

Thankfully, the book of Revelation has its own outline, which we can use to further understand its message. In Revelation 1:19, John the Revelator is told, "Write the things which thou *hast seen,* and the things which *are,* and the things which *shall be hereafter*" (emphases added). This statement could serve as the mentioned outline for the entire book, as follows:

- Revelation 1 consists of "the things which [John saw]." This first chapter is centered on Jesus Christ.
- In Revelation 2–3, John "[wrote of] the things which [were]" in his time. These chapters contain letters written to the seven churches in Asia.
- In Revelation 4–22, John "[wrote of] the things which shall be [after his time]." In these chapters are the writings concerning the seven seals and information from the beginning of the days of Adam and Enoch down to and after the final judgment.

John the Revelator truly saw events from the beginning of time until the days after the Millennium. Elder Gerald N. Lund wrote:

> The basic structure of the vision is chronological. After seeing the Father and the Son in heaven (Rev. 4–5) . . . [John] sees the first five seals (or first five thousand years of history) in rapid-fire . . . form. Then he sees the opening of the sixth seal, which includes the restoration of the gospel. (Rev. 6:12–7:17)
>
> After that, John sees the seventh period of a thousand years, with great judgments poured out upon the earth, including Armageddon (see Rev. 8–9, 11, 16) . . . [and] the utter overthrow of Babylon (see Rev. 17–18) [to] make way for the Second Coming . . . Immediately following that, John sees Satan bound and Christ reigning for a thousand years (see Rev. 20:1–6), [then] a last great battle between the forces of righteousness and evil (see Rev. 20:7-10), and the final judgment (Rev. 20:11–15).

Finally, a new heaven and a new earth are brought forth
(see Rev. 21:1–22:5).[16]

To read John's reaction to those events is priceless; Revelation chapter
22 gives good insight to John's attitude after seeing all of these dramatic
events. Revelation 22:17 reads, "And the Spirit and the bride say, Come.
And let him that heareth say, Come. And let him that is athirst come.
And whosoever will, let him take of the water of life freely." Revelation
22:20 adds, "He which testifieth these things saith, Surely I come quickly.
Amen. Even so, come, Lord Jesus." After seeing all of the destruction and
plagues and wars and battles and calamities, John's invitation is, "Come,
Lord Jesus!" He appears to be excited for Jesus's triumphant return; this
should fill our hearts with hope.

Sterling W. Sill, an assistant to the Quorum of the Twelve Apostles,
explained concerning the book of Revelation:

> The most often mentioned event in the entire Bible is
> that wonderful, yet awful experience that we will have
> when Jesus Christ shall come to judge our world. There
> are many important gospel doctrines mentioned in
> the Bible only briefly, and some not at all. [Being born
> again] is mentioned in the Bible nine times; baptism is
> mentioned 52 times, repentance is mentioned 89 times,
> but the Second Coming of Christ is mentioned over 1,500
> times in the Old Testament and 300 times in the New
> Testament. If God thought this subject that important,
> He must have wanted us to *do something about it*.[17]

Let's talk about the author of Revelation. He is sometimes called
"John the Beloved" or "John the Revelator." Doctrine and Covenants
7:3–6 states that John's words would be heard before many nations. As
an author of five books of the Bible, which is one of the most widely
distributed books in the world,[18] John's impact within nations as
prophesied in Doctrine and Covenants 7 is valid.

---

16 Gerald N. Lund, "Seeing the Book of Revelation As a Book of Revelation," *Ensign*,
Dec. 1987, 52.
17 *Doctrines of the Gospel Student Manual*, (2000), 100–103 (see also Sterling W. Sill,
*Ensign*, May 1966, 18).
18 Craig Glenday, *Guinness World Records*, (New York: Bantam, 2014), 113.

The issue of John's current status has been argued for years, some scholars saying that he was taken from the Isle of Patmos and eventually died and was buried in Ephesus (modern-day Turkey). Others believe that he was translated and is alive upon the earth today. The Prophet Joseph Smith made record of a conversation between him and Oliver Cowdery about this matter. "A difference of opinion arising between us about the account of John the Apostle, mentioned in the New Testament, as to whether he died or continued to live, we mutually agreed to settle it by the Urim and Thummim" (*History of the Church,* 1:35–36).[19] The Prophet Joseph Smith concluded that "John the Revelator was . . . among the Ten Tribes of Israel . . . to prepare them for their return from their long dispersion."[20]

Following is an overview of the timeline of events revealed to John, along with the chapters corresponding to each event. This bird's-eye view will help you keep the sequence straight as you study. As you read each chapter in Revelation, look for these events generally:

| EVENT | REFERENCE |
|---|---|
| Pre-Earth Life | Revelation 12 |
| Adam and Eve —Birth of Christ | Revelation 6 |
| Jesus's and John's Mortal Ministries | Revelation 1–3, 10 |
| The Great Apostasy | Revelation 6, 13 |
| The Restoration | Revelation 14 |
| Signs of the Times (and Adam-ondi-Ahman) | Revelation 7–9 (and latter-day revelation) |
| Armageddon | Revelation 16 |
| Appearance in Jerusalem | Revelation 11 |
| Righteous Rewarded | Revelation 15 |
| Wicked Destroyed | Revelation 16–18 |
| Jesus's Appearance to the World | Revelation 19 |
| The Millennium and Final Judgement | Revelation 20 |
| The Celestialized Earth | Revelation 4–5, 21–22 |

Now that we've learned about Revelation and its author and have seen its overview, let's begin our study, looking briefly at each vision and then spending time discovering principles for application from each prophecy.

---

19 See also 3 Ne. 28:1–7; here, it is recorded that the Nephite disciples received the same translated status as John.

20 *History of the Church* vol. 1, 176.

## *Revelation 1*
### JESUS CHRIST

RECALL THE OUTLINE PROVIDED BY Revelation 1:19. The first chapter is centered on Jesus Christ. If you were to open your scriptures to Revelation 1 and then close your eyes and point your finger to any verse in that chapter, you will most likely land on a verse or a symbol about the Savior.

Interestingly, Revelation 1:1 reads, "The Revelation of Jesus Christ, which God gave unto him, to shew unto his servants things which must shortly come to pass; and he sent and *signified it* by his angel unto his servant John" (emphasis added). The Greek word for *signify* is *sémeion*, which is derived from *sémainó*. When considered together, these words mean *to show by signs or tokens*.[21] An angel would reveal himself to be a true angel in this manner according to revelation given in Doctrine and Covenants 129:4–5. A corollary to this principle is found in Acts 1:1–3, as delineated below.

1. Jesus began both to do and teach,
2. Until the day in which he was taken up, after that he through the Holy Ghost had given commandments unto the apostles whom he had chosen:
3. To whom also he shewed himself alive after his passion by many infallible proofs.

The Greek word for *infallible proofs* is *tekmérion*, meaning *to show or prove by a sure sign*.[22]

---

21 "Sémainó," "Sémeion" (4591, 4592, respectively). In *Strong's Concordance*, accessed June 19, 2017, biblehub.com/greek/1404.htm.

22 "Tekmérion" (5039). In *Strong's Concordance*, accessed June 19, 2017, biblehub.com/greek/1404.htm.

Below are a few verses and phrases from Revelation 1 that describe the Savior in John's vision:

- He is "the faithful witness," "the first begotten of the dead," and "the [ruler] of the kings of the earth" (verse 5).
- He loves us and He "washed us from our sins in his own blood" (verse 5).
- He "[has] made us kings and priests unto God and his Father" (verse 6).
- He was "clothed with a garment down to the foot, and girt about the paps with a golden girdle" (verse 13).
- "His head and his hairs were white like wool, as white as snow; and his eyes were as a flame of fire" (verse 14).
- "[H]is feet [were] like unto fine brass, as if they burned in a furnace; and his voice as the sound of many waters" (verse 15).
- "[H]e had in his right hand seven stars: and out of his mouth went a sharp two-edged sword: and his countenance was as the sun shineth in his strength" (verse 16).

Great numbers of people on our planet are Christians; approximately one-third of the people on Earth gather to celebrate the Resurrection at Easter; nearly half of our world's population celebrates His birth at Christmas. It's absolutely remarkable that, despite the many centuries that have passed, the number of believers has continued to increase. In the early church, there were not many copies of the Bible (they didn't exist until about 300 years after Jesus's death), and when He died, very few people believed His message. So what made Jesus's teachings so timeless (and unique)? Surely it was the doctrine and witnesses of His death and His Resurrection. It wasn't His teaching, doctrine, or charisma that converted the small band of believers. After all, Peter just wanted to go fishing after Jesus died! The single converting moment for the disciples came as they visited the empty tomb. From this point on, these men (and women) boldly preached and unabashedly taught in the streets and in houses. And interestingly, they didn't preach and teach about His persona or His parables or personality; they almost exclusively preached about one fact: His Resurrection. And John, the author of the book of Revelation, was a special and firsthand witness of the risen, living Lord (see John 20:1–20).

Notice in the Joseph Smith Translation of Revelation 1:7 that the Lord is "in the clouds with ten *thousands* of his Saints." The number 10,000 was among the largest used by the ancients; it likely represents a large (and based on John's pluralization, *ten thousands*, possibly innumerable) number of people. What a message of hope, that we too might be among the throng if we prepare for His return and remain faithful!

One title for Jesus Christ that John shared from which we can draw personal application is found in Revelation 1:8. Here, Christ is called "Alpha and Omega." Elder Jeffrey R. Holland wrote about this title:

> These letters from the Greek suggest the universal role of Jesus from the beginning of the world to its end. But he ought to be Alpha and Omega in the particular as well . . .
>
> In every choice we make, he ought to be our point of reckoning, our charted course, our only harbor ahead. He should be for us individually what he is for all men collectively—the very brackets of existence, the compass of our privilege. We should not stray outside him.[23]

While it is appropriate and good to praise and thank God for generalities such as our clothes and our job and our car and our health and safety, worshiping Him means something very different. Worship of God—making Him our Alpha and Omega—means that even if we don't have a job or great health or a perfect house, we still give Him praise; we choose to worship Him not for what He's done but simply for who He is. He indeed is the beginning of faith, the beginning of hope, the beginning of life—and He is the end of bitterness, death, and sorrow.

**AN APPLICATION**

*Do you feel that the Savior is the center of your worship and the center of your life?*

Why did John use so many symbols? Joseph Fielding McConkie wrote:

> Symbols are the timeless and universal language in which God, in his wisdom, has chosen to teach his gospel and bear witness of his Son. They are the language of the scriptures, the language of revelation, the language of the Spirit, the language of faith. They are a language common to the Saints of all generations.[24]

23 Jeffrey R. Holland, "Whom say Ye that I Am?," *Ensign*, Sept. 1974, 7.
24 Joseph Fielding McConkie, *Gospel Symbolism* (Salt Lake City: Bookcraft, 1985), 1.

Notice the symbolism of the right hand in Revelation 1:16–17: "And he had in his *right hand* seven stars . . . And he laid his *right hand* upon me" (emphases added). The right hand is the covenant hand,[25] the hand of favor and honor and a symbol of power; we use our right hand to sustain, to take and pass the sacrament, and in everyday handshakes.

The Lord is holding seven stars in His right hand. It appears, based on the context of the next two chapters wherein John is writing letters to the seven leaders of the seven churches, that the Lord is symbolically holding the leaders of His seven churches (branches or congregations) in His right hand.

Who are these modern-day *stars*, or leaders filled with light, being held in the hand of the Lord? The modern-day stars of our churches may be bishops and stake presidents. Jesus told His disciples in the Americas, "Therefore, hold up your light that it may shine unto the world. Behold I am the light which ye shall hold up—that which ye have seen me do" (3 Ne. 18:24). Our modern-day righteous priesthood holders carry the same light. Just as stars would guide mariners in ancient times, priesthood leaders provide guidance for us.

Admittedly, some people have had personal issues with priesthood leaders in our modern day: a bishop who didn't handle something well or perhaps a stake president who came across a bit abruptly on a matter. However, the mantle carried by these good volunteer leaders is powerful and their closeness to Christ is divine. The Lord knows and loves His priesthood leaders. He knows and is certainly close to the stars of His church.

President Dieter F. Uchtdorf taught:

> [T]o be perfectly frank, there have been times when members or leaders in the Church have simply made mistakes. There may have been things said or done that were not in harmony with our values, principles, or doctrine.
>
> I suppose the Church would be perfect only if it were run by perfect beings. God is perfect, and His doctrine is pure. But He works through us—His imperfect children—and imperfect people make mistakes. . . .

---

25 See Joseph Fielding Smith, *Doctrines of Salvation* vol. 3 (Salt Lake City: Bookcraft, 1954), 518–519; Joseph Fielding Smith, *Answers to Gospel Questions*, vol. 1 (Salt Lake City: Deseret Book, 1957), 77–78.

It is unfortunate that some have stumbled because of mistakes made by men. But in spite of this, the eternal truth of the restored gospel found in The Church of Jesus Christ of Latter-day Saints is not tarnished, diminished, or destroyed.

As an Apostle of the Lord Jesus Christ and as one who has seen firsthand the councils and workings of this Church, I bear solemn witness that no decision of significance affecting this Church or its members is ever made without earnestly seeking the inspiration, guidance, and approbation of our Eternal Father. This is the Church of Jesus Christ. God will not allow His Church to drift from its appointed course or fail to fulfill its divine destiny.[26]

## AN APPLICATION

*How is your relationship with your priesthood leaders? Are you sustaining your priesthood leaders, despite their human imperfections?*

Let's explore one more application from this first chapter. In Revelation 1:10, John tells us that he "was in the Spirit on the Lord's day." Historically, Sabbath day remembrance and observance has seen at least three dramatic shifts throughout the course of time:

| | REMEMBRANCE | OBSERVANCE |
|---|---|---|
| **OLD TESTAMENT** | The Creation of the earth and Israel's redemption from Egypt | Prepare on the sixth day and remember on the Sabbath day. |
| **NEW TESTAMENT** | The Creation of the earth and Israel's redemption from Egypt | Prepare on the sixth day and rest from all labors. |
| **LATTER DAYS** | Jesus's death and Resurrection and our deliverance from sin | Prepare on Saturday and keep the Sabbath holy by following Jesus's example. |

Seeking and then being *in the Spirit* through our activities on the Sabbath is a wonderful goal for Latter-day Saints. Elder Dallin H. Oaks, addressing appropriate and inappropriate Sabbath Day activities, counseled:

[Teachers should] not provide a list of *dos* and *don'ts* for keeping the Sabbath day holy. Once a teacher has taught the

---

26 Dieter F. Uchtdorf, "Come, Join with Us," *Ensign*, Nov. 2013.

doctrine and the associated principles from the scriptures and the living prophets, such specific applications or rules are the responsibility of individuals and families.[27]

So, in order for us to be *in the Spirit on the Lord's day*, what are some Sabbath day principles that help determine what is appropriate and what may not be appropriate for Sabbath day activities and observance? Consider these:

- Does it bring me closer to God?
- Is it unselfish?
- Does it keep me unspotted from the world? (See D&C 59:9–10).
- Does it prevent someone else from keeping the Sabbath day holy?

By way of application, recall that the children of Israel spent 400 years working seven days a week as slaves. Their value, as perceived by the pharaohs, was based on how much they could produce. They seemed to have been treated like machines for centuries. Can you imagine the joy they must have felt when the first Sunday came along after they were released from bondage? It's no wonder the Lord counseled them (and us) to do such things on Sunday as reflect on the Savior, remember and renew covenants, revive ourselves, and relax. It's important to remember that we are not machines; we need rest, and the best day to find divine rest is on the Sabbath. As we seek the Savior on Sundays and throughout the week, we can apply the symbols of the Savior found in Revelation 1.

## AN APPLICATION

*Do you prepare for and strive to keep the Sabbath day holy?*

---

27 Dallin H. Oaks, "Gospel Teaching," *Ensign*, Nov. 1999.

## *Revelation 2-3*
### SEVEN LETTERS TO SEVEN CHURCHES

RECALL FROM JOHN'S OUTLINE IN Revelation 1:19 that Revelation 2 and 3 are centered on the seven letters written to the seven churches in Asia. In each of his letters, John invites the people to come unto Christ. As we study these letters, we may find it ironic that many of the troubles that were plaguing the ancient church are still plaguing our wards today!

An article in the *Ensign*, written by Jay M. Todd, reads:

> Perhaps few chapters in scripture afford such insightful glimpses into the spirit of the Lord's judgment as do the first three chapters of Revelation. The Lord's appraisal of the members' faithfulness, endurance, patience, charity, and service—and their inactivity, cooling of love, tolerance of wickedness and false doctrines, lukewarmness, self-satisfaction, worldliness, and lack of zeal in his cause—have served for generations to motivate thoughtful readers to evaluate thoroughly their lifestyle.[28]

These messages were written by John in A.D. 95 when the Church of Jesus Christ was about 66 years old.[29] The church had experienced growth despite intense persecution. Under the rule of Rome, records show that thousands of Christians were slain by crucifixion, burned to death, and thrown to wild animals. In addition, corruption was springing up in the church. The Lord's concerns for the seven churches are evident in John's letters to each congregation as delineated in the following outline:

28 Jay M. Todd, "The Seven Cities of Revelation," *Ensign*, Aug. 1976.
29 See "The Revelation of Jesus Christ Unto His Servant, John." In *The Life and Teachings of Jesus Christ and His Apostles*, 2nd ed. (Salt Lake City: The Church of Jesus Christ of Latter-day Saints, 1979), 448–55.

Revelation 2:1–7
   Ephesus: The church that had forsaken its first love (Rev 2:4)
Revelation 2:8–11
   Smyrna: The church that would be persecuted (Rev 2:10)
Revelation 2:12–17
   Pergamos: The church that needed to repent (Rev 2:16)
Revelation 2:18–29
   Thyatira: The church that had a false prophetess (Rev 2:20)
Revelation 3:1–6
   Sardis: The church that needed to be watchful (Rev 3:2)
Revelation 3:7–13
   Philadelphia: The church that had endured patiently (Rev 3:10)
Revelation 3:14–22
   Laodicea: The church that was "lukewarm" (Rev 3:16)

The scriptures are replete with the Lord's voice of counsel and chastening, and these chapters certainly provide reasons for the Lord's concern for His children, as well as for His divine correction. Certainly His desire was to help the saints in these ancient cities (and also us, as readers) to repent and make course corrections. The following scriptures reflect the Lord's love for those He chastens:

- Proverbs 13:24: He that spareth his rod hateth his son: but he that loveth him chasteneth him betimes.
- Psalms 94:12: Blessed is the man whom thou chastenest, O LORD, and teachest him out of thy law.
- Doctrine and Covenants 90:36: But verily I say unto you, that I, the Lord, will contend with Zion, and plead with her strong ones, and chasten her until she overcomes and is clean before me.

Elder D. Todd Christofferson taught:

Divine chastening has at least three purposes: (1) to persuade us to repent, (2) to refine and sanctify us, and (3) at times to redirect our course in life to what God knows is a better path. . . . Let us pray for His love-inspired correction.[30]

30 D. Todd Christofferson, "As Many as I Love, I Rebuke and Chasten," *Ensign*, May 2011, 98.

Being cognizant of and feeling deeply when corrected, chastened, and rebuked are indications of being close to the Holy Ghost. Saints who respond quickly to the urgings of the Spirit and who are pained and seek repentance when the Spirit chastens them for poor choices are on the pathway of discipleship. The wicked, in contrast, who quickly dismiss the discomfort that comes from divine chastening, reject those promptings to repent, and sadly continue in their accustomed way. Alma 62:41 illustrates this very clearly; in that passage, there are two different responses by two groups of people to the same war-time chastening:

> But behold, because of the exceedingly great length of the war between the Nephites and the Lamanites many had become hardened, because of the exceedingly great length of the war; and many were softened because of their afflictions, insomuch that they did humble themselves before God, even in the depth of humility.

In Alma 5, the prophet Alma asks more than forty questions, challenging readers to examine themselves, reminding readers of the many possible ways in which correction can be made. We certainly each need to take a careful inventory of our life and our performance to be better prepared for Christ's coming. As Elder Neal A. Maxwell taught:

> Why not, therefore, take full advantage of the . . . tutoring questions and the emerging and instructive one-liners from the Lord? . . . [T]hese questions are full of generic insights and needed directions for us.[31]

### AN APPLICATION

*Do you feel chastened by the Spirit? (If so, it's actually a great sign that you are sensitive to the Holy Ghost.)*

We will now explore the letters written to the seven church branches, looking for principles for application from each message.

---

31 Neal A. Maxwell, *Men and Women of Christ* (Salt Lake City: Bookcraft, 1991), 110–12.

## TO THE CHURCH IN EPHESUS (REV. 2:1–7)

Ephesus was the capital in western Asia Minor (modern-day Turkey). Its Temple of Diana was considered one of the seven wonders of the world. Many of the most eminent orators and philosophers of the world spent time in Ephesus. Its church was founded by Paul (see Acts 18:19–21, 19:1–10), who spent about three years there—longer than he spent in any other place. In its day, Ephesus housed the largest outdoor theatre in the world, capable of containing 50,000 spectators. It hosted fights between wild beasts and between men and beasts.

In Revelation 2:4, the Lord reproaches the church at Ephesus for having left its first love. How does a person leave their first love? An analogy to fog may help illuminate this principle. According to The Weather Guys, one cubic inch of fog contains tiny drops of water measuring about one-thousandth of an inch. In just one cubic mile, there are about 56,000 gallons of water.[32] With this information, it's easy to comprehend how these minute water droplets can blind us when they settle over our lands. By application, it appears that some of the Ephesian saints in John's day had gotten lost in the fog of life. Although their gospel fog may have seemed negligible, it was enough to distract them from the gospel path.

An example of leaving one's first love is found in the life of Peter the Apostle. Recall that following the Crucifixion of Christ, Peter had decided to return to his occupation as a fisherman. In John 21:11, Peter catches 153 fish with the Lord's help. Elder Jeffrey R. Holland taught a beautiful application of a principle, using Peter as an example. After asking Peter if he loved Him, the Savior in essence said:

> Peter, why are you here? Why are we back on this same shore, by these same nets, having this same conversation? Wasn't it obvious then and isn't it obvious now that if I want fish, I can get fish? What I need, Peter, are disciples— and I need them forever. I need someone to feed my sheep and save my lambs. I need someone to preach my gospel and defend my faith. I need someone who loves me, truly, truly loves me, and loves what our Father in Heaven has commissioned me to do. Ours is not a feeble message. It

---

32 "How Much Condensed Liquid Water Is in a Cubic Mile of Fog and Clouds?," *The Why Files: The Science Behind the News*, June 19, 2017, whyfiles.org/2011/how-much-condensed-liquid-water-is-in-a-cubic-mile-of-fog-and-clouds.

is not a fleeting task. It is not hapless; it is not hopeless; it is not to be consigned to the ash heap of history. It is the work of Almighty God, and it is to change the world. So, Peter, for the second and presumably the last time, I am asking you to leave all this and to go teach and testify, labor and serve loyally until the day in which they will do to you exactly what they did to me.[33]

Love of God is always coupled with *loyalty* to God. We mustn't quit when our discipleship is put to the test. Although we may be tempted to put on an *I'm going fishing* T-shirt and throw in the proverbial towel from time to time, we instead should exchange *that* T-shirt for one that reads, *I'm going to feed sheep!* And instead of throwing in the towel, we should use that towel to wipe the sweat from our brow and then get back to working in the Lord's vineyard. We should take inventory of our lives and identify areas that need improvement.

## AN APPLICATION

*Is the Savior your first and true love? Do you have any* fish *in your life? Consider setting some goals to show Him that your love for Him is much richer than* 153 fish, *and that He is truly your first love.*

## TO THE CHURCH IN SMYRNA (REV. 2:8–11)

In Revelation 2:9, John wrote to the church in Smyrna,[34] "I know the blasphemy of them which say they are Jews, and are not, but are the synagogue of Satan." An example of Smyrna's blasphemy is found in the story of Polycarp, a young pupil of John, who was a prominent leader in the church of Smyrna. Here he ultimately suffered martyrdom in A.D. 155.[35] Unwilling to bow to Caesar and worship him, Polycarp was tried in the presence of a mob before the governor and was told to curse Christ. His reply was simple: "Eighty and six years have I served him, and He hath done me no wrong: how then can I blaspheme my king who saved me?" The governor persisted, "I have wild beasts; if thou wilt not change

---

33 Jeffrey R. Holland, "The First Great Commandment," *Ensign*, Nov. 2012.

34 Smyrna, established by Alexander the Great in 333 B.C., housed the largest marketplace in the world. The city's name means *myrrh* (a resin used in embalming the dead). See Ray Reynolds, "The Churches of Christ in the New Testament" (Lesson 12 in Bible Class Series, 2011; gulfshoreschurchofchrist.org).

35 *New Testament Student Manual* (IRI, 2014).

thy mind I will throw thee to them." Polycarp replied, "Bid them be
brought." Again the governor spoke, "As thou despisest the beasts . . . I
will make thee to be destroyed by fire." Polycarp courageously answered,
"[Why delayest thou?] Bring what thou wilt." The governor's messenger
instructed the assembled multitude to burn him alive. Timber and
kindling were brought and Polycarp was thrown to the flames.[36]

The blasphemy of those who say they are faithful to the Savior but
whose actions tell otherwise is dangerous. For example, my former stake
president is a convert to the church. When he was fifteen years of age, his
friends invited him to attend seminary, and slowly the seeds of testimony
began to grow in his heart. A short while later he was baptized. Before
his baptism, he was asked if there was anything that made him hesitant
to join the Church. His answer was instructive. He said that he found it
ironic that while attending church, he noticed leaders imploring Church
members to hold family home evening, family scripture study, and family
prayer but then he noticed that very few members seemed to go home and
actually engage in those activities. He did not want to seem judgmental,
but he felt that many Church members were a bit hypocritical in their
religiosity. They could talk the talk on Sunday but weren't as eager to walk
the walk once they exited the doors of the church.

Jesus taught this principle to His followers, commanding them in
Matthew 5:13 to be "the salt of the earth." Salt, as we know, prevents
bacteria from growing; Jesus may have been implying that as Christians,
we are to prevent cultural decay. If salt remains in a shaker, it isn't able
to perform its function. The politicians, educators, and lawyers aren't
the salt: we Christians are the salt, and we've been commanded to help
prevent cultural decay.

In addition to preventing decay, salt also creates thirst and is flavorful.
Have you ever had popcorn without salt? Or a French fry without salt? Food
tastes so much better with salt. As the "salt of the earth," we are to create a
flavor and hunger for Jesus Christ. That is, we should be so "salty" that people
become thirsty and eventually beg for the living water that Christ offers.

In application, are you salt at your job? Or are you just like every other
worker? Is there anything unique about how you conduct yourself at work?

---

36 *"Martyrium Polycarpi*, or The Letter of the Smyrnaeans." In *Documents Illustrative
of the History of the Church*, 2nd ed. Henry Bettenson (ed.). Oxford: Oxford
University Press, 1967, 9–12; as quoted by Alexander Morrison, *Feed My Sheep:
Leadership Ideas for Latter-day Shepherds* (Salt Lake City: Deseret Book, 1992), 165.

This means that if, for example, you are a doctor, you're not *just* a doctor. You're God's representative in the medical field so others can see how God would treat sick people if He were on the earth. If you're a teacher, you're not *just* a teacher. You're God's representative in the classroom so others can see what God is like when He teaches a lesson. If you are a lawyer, you're not *just* a lawyer. You're God's representative in the courtroom so others can see how God would handle people with legal issues if He were in the courtroom. And moms? You're not *just* a mom. You're God's representative in the home so children can see what God is like when He raises a family.

Like Polycarp, we should be salt and light "at all times and in all things, and in all places" (Mosiah 18:9) so as to avoid the appearance of hypocrisy. We, like the Church members living in Smyrna, may be persecuted for a season because of our testimonies, but being true to our faith and consistent with our beliefs will bring bounteous blessings from above.

**AN APPLICATION**

*Is there any hypocrisy in your life? Is there anything in your actions that contradicts your covenants?*

**TO THE CHURCH IN PERGAMOS (REV. 2:12–17)**

We learn a bit about the city of Pergamos from Revelation 2:12–13: "Pergamos . . . thou dwellest . . . where Satan's seat is."[37] In Revelation 2:17, the Lord invites these Saints to look beyond this false and satanic throne and to seek for hidden manna. Manna, as you may recall, was the food that Israel received from heaven while they wandered in the wilderness (see Ex. 16:35). Later, in the New Testament (John 6:32), the Savior referred to himself as "true bread from heaven" and taught in John chapter 6:

48. I am [the] bread of life.
49. Your fathers did eat manna in the wilderness, and are dead.
50. This is the bread which cometh down from heaven, that a man may eat thereof, and not die.
51. I am the living bread which came down from heaven: if any man eat of this bread, he shall live for ever.

---

37 "Satan's seat" as used here may have referred to the altar at Pergamos (see "Revelation 1–3." In *New Testament Student Manual* [IRI, 2014]). The residents of Pergamos had erected an enormous altar dedicated to the god Zeus, which had the appearance of a throne and stood on a hill overlooking the city.

The phrase *hidden manna* may also refer to truths that are revealed in the temple, as Revelation 2:17 has obvious temple connotations: "[I] will give him a white stone, and in the stone a new name written." The Lord, through the Prophet Joseph Smith and referring directly to this passage, revealed, "Then the white stone mentioned in Revelation 2:17, will become a Urim and Thummim to each individual who receives one, whereby things pertaining to a higher order of kingdoms will be made known" (D&C 130:10).

One purpose of the Lord's Old Testament manna miracle was to teach the people of Israel that one "[does] not live by bread only, but on every word that proceedeth out of the mouth of the LORD" (Deut. 8:3).[38] Like the Israelites in the desert, Jesus was totally dependent on the provisions of His Heavenly Father while in the wilderness of temptation (see Matt. 4:11).

An application of *manna* is the sacrament we partake of each week,[39] officiated by young priesthood holders.[40] If we think about it, our sacrament is a reminder of our dependence on God. Each week we attend a memorial service for the Good Shepherd. We have pallbearers, or deacons, who transport the body, or bread; we have morticians, or teachers, who carefully prepare the body; and we invite young men (priests) to offer a family prayer; all in an effort to help point our minds to the *living* bread, Jesus Christ, and His Resurrection three short days after His death.

During the sacrament we should examine our lives and ponder the Savior's Atonement and His role as our Savior. We do not need to be perfect in order to partake of the sacrament, but we should have a spirit of humility in our hearts. The sacrament can become a source of strength

---

38 Jesus, while fasting, referred to this statement to refuse Satan's suggestion that He turn stones into bread (see Matt. 4:4).

39 John 6:11 records that Jesus "took the loaves; and when he had given thanks, he distributed to the disciples, and the disciples to them that were set down; and likewise of the fishes as much as they would." Later, during the last supper, Jesus took the bread, gave thanks, and gave it to His Apostles to eat (see Matt. 26:26, Mark 14:22, Luke 22:19, 1 Cor. 11:23–24). Certainly there is possible symbolism between the sacrament and manna.

40 It is interesting to note that the term "preparatory priesthood" is not found in the standard works. However, we know that in addition to preparing young men to receive the Melchizedek Priesthood, the Aaronic Priesthood and its ordinances prepare Saints to enter into greater covenants (through the Melchizedek Priesthood), which in turn brings the Saints into the presence of the Father.

and an opportunity to rededicate ourselves to living the gospel. And as we partake of it, we are promised that His Spirit may be with us always (see D&C 20:77, 79). The reception of the Spirit by partaking of our modern-day manna can indeed act much like these white stones mentioned in Revelation 2:17; the Holy Ghost can be our guide and our source of inspiration as we worthily partake of the sacrament each Sunday.

## AN APPLICATION

*How well do you prepare to take the sacrament each Sunday?*

## TO THE CHURCH IN THYATIRA (REV. 2:18–29)

"I have a few things against thee," reads Revelation 2:20, "because thou sufferest that woman Jezebel, which calleth herself a prophetess, to teach and to seduce my servants to commit fornication." In Thyatira,[41] permissive Christians allowed immorality into their city, typified by a woman named Jezebel; further, many claimed that the grace of God freed them from having to obey His commandments, including His command to remain pure and virtuous.

The first Jezebel appears in 1 Kings 16. Here, it is recorded that she married Ahab, king of Israel. As a daughter of this perverse kingdom, she was raised in an atmosphere where immorality was a path to power and influence, and she completely subdued and dominated Ahab. Ahab permitted Jezebel's persecution of God's prophets (1 Kgs. 18:4); he failed to silence Jezebel's threat on Elijah's life (1 Kgs. 19:2). By Jezebel's influence, he, along with many Israelites, left the worship of God for Baal and Ashtaroth. The prophet Elijah lamented that only a few men in the entire nation were not swayed by her control (1 Kgs. 19:18).

The *spirit of Jezebel* could be compared to a controlling spirit working through the lusts of the flesh and the eyes. Consider the example of a fire burning in a fireplace. Fires are warm and cozy, but, for safety's sake, they belong in a fireplace. Sexual intimacy is much the same way. It is a blessing and ordained by God, but it belongs in the right place, between a married man and woman. The law of chastity keeps our God-given passions in their proper places, despite Jezebel-like temptations. Romans 13:14

---

41 Thyatira was a trading town that was famous for its dyeing of cloth. One of Thyatira's residents was Lydia, a seller of purple, or rather of cloth dyed with this color (see Acts 16:14). Through the preaching of the Apostle Paul at Philippi, Lydia and her household became converted. Lydia may have been an emissary of God to first carry the gospel throughout her native town.

reminds us, "But put ye on the Lord Jesus Christ, and make not provision for the flesh, to fulfil the lusts thereof." We should make no provisions for her—no opportunity for Jezebel's enticements.

Recall from Revelation 2:20 that Thyatira's Jezebel aimed "to teach and to seduce [the Lord's] servants to commit fornication." Likening this passage to our day, do we have any modern-day Jezebels in our society? Do we have people (both women and men) in our modern world whose goal it is to seduce the servants of God to immorality? If we look at modern-day movies and other media, for example, it is clear that we indeed have many modern-day Jezebels. The city of Thyatira had one Jezebel; we certainly have many in our society today.

In Revelation 2:23, the Lord declares that He "searcheth the *reins and hearts*" (emphasis added). "The word *reins* literally means kidneys . . . [which] signified strength and vigor. [This] phrase . . . [means] that the Lord knows all things about the inner man, his strengths and weaknesses, his character and emotions."[42] Indeed He will search us and will detect if we have any unworthy feelings toward the Jezebels in our life.

The Joseph Smith Translation teaches that those who overcame Jezebel did it "with the word of God" (Joseph Smith Translation Rev. 2:26–27). Studying the word of God, coupled with prayer, leads us away from temptation. Helaman 3 teaches:

> 29. Yea, we see that whosoever will may lay hold upon the word of God, which is quick and powerful, which shall divide asunder all the cunning and the snares and the wiles of the devil, and lead the man of Christ in a strait and narrow course across that everlasting gulf of misery which is prepared to engulf the wicked—
>
> 30. And land their souls, yea, their immortal souls, at the right hand of God in the kingdom of heaven, to sit down with Abraham, and Isaac, and with Jacob, and with all our holy fathers, to go no more out.

Scripture study and prayer keep us focused on our Savior. Having a vision and understanding of Him is key to our gospel success.

Florence Chadwick, a swimmer from my hometown of San Diego, California, was the first female to swim the English Channel in both directions. She then attempted to complete a marathon swim from Catalina

---

42 *The Life and Teachings of Jesus Christ and His Apostles*, 2nd ed. (Salt Lake City: The Church of Jesus Christ of Latter-day Saints, 1979), 452.

Island to Southern California in the early 1950s. Spotters who flanked her in small boats watched for sharks and were prepared to come to her rescue if she got injured or fatigued—her mother was among them. A thick fog set in about fifteen hours into her swim, and Florence, doubting her ability, told her mother that she didn't think she could finish. Florence could not see the coastline through the fog; after one more hour, she asked to be pulled from the channel. During the boat ride back to the California coast, Florence found that she had been just one mile from her goal when she had stopped swimming. She tried again two months later. Despite the same thick fog setting in, she reached her destination. She said of her experience that she had kept a mental image of the shoreline during her swim.[43, 44]

By way of application, sometimes people give in to Jezebel's temptations because they can't see well and have gotten lost in the fog of life, such as in Lehi's vision of the Tree of Life (see 1 Ne. 8). When people lose sight or vision of their destination because of the temptation-laden fogs of mortality, they experience premature gospel withdrawal. "For now we see through a glass, darkly," reads 1 Corinthians 13:12, and Proverbs 29:18 adds, "Where there is no vision, the people perish." Maintaining our vision as we swim through the waters of mortality is essential if we are to make wise choices to combat the Jezebels of our day and finish our race on Earth.

One invitation from the Lord found in the story of the saints of Thyatira is to stay focused on our ultimate destination by fleeing from modern-day Jezebels, avoiding their temptations through the study of His word.

### AN APPLICATION

*Are there any Jezebels (male or female) in your life? Are there any temptations that you have allowed to enter into your life? Do you feel that your study of the scriptures is enough to overcome powerful Jezebel temptations?*

### TO THE CHURCH IN SARDIS (REV. 3:1–6)

Despite being among the first cities in that part of the world that welcomed the preaching of the Apostle John, the church at Sardis was described as being "dead" (Rev. 3:1).[45] It appeared to be spiritually lifeless. There is

---

43 "Florence Chadwick," *Wikipedia*, accessed Jun. 6, 2017, https://en.wikipedia.org/wiki/Florence_Chadwick.

44 "Queen of the Channel: Florence Chadwick," *Channel Swimming Association*, accessed Jun. 6, 2017, www.queenofthechannel.com/florence-chadwick.

45 As the capital of the ancient kingdom of Lydia, Sardis was famous for its golden sand, was one of the most splendid and opulent cities of the East, and was famous for its high standards of living and exorbitant ways of life.

no indication of persecution or trouble from outside forces like the other churches had to battle. Neither, in contrast to some of the other churches, was there any mention of heresy within it, as far as the records show. Things seemed to be peaceful. But something was wrong on the inside.

In Revelation 3:3, John wrote, "Remember therefore how thou hast received and heard." In the scriptures we are often instructed, counseled, and commanded to *remember*. The Saints in Sardis struggled to remember the teachings they had previously received; we too must be careful not to forget what we know is true. The gospel provides a tool in the words of the sacrament prayers to help us accomplish this goal. The word *remember* is repeated each and every Sunday in our sacrament prayers. Susan L. Warner, while serving as a member of the Primary General Presidency, counseled:

> This repeated invitation emphasizes the important connection between our recollection of spiritual feelings in our past and our faithfulness in the present. Satan wants us to be slow to remember what we have received and heard . . . He wants us to minimize and even forget the quiet witnesses of the Spirit that have told us who we really are.[46]

In the Book of Mormon, there are over 240 instances of the word *remember*. President Spencer W. Kimball said:

> When you look in the dictionary for the most important word, do you know what it is? It could be "remember." Because all of [us] have made covenants . . . our greatest need is to remember. That is why everyone goes to sacrament meeting every Sabbath day—to take the sacrament and listen to the priests pray that [we] "may always remember him and keep his commandments which he has given [us]." . . . "Remember" is the word.[47]

Notice the blessing that comes to those who remember. In Revelation 3:4 we read, "[A] few . . . have not defiled their garments; and they shall

---

46 Susan L. Warner, "Remember How Thou Hast Received and Heard," *Ensign*, May 1996.
47 Spencer W. Kimball, "Circles of Exaltation," address to CES religious educators, Brigham Young University, Jun. 28, 1968, 8.

walk with me in white: for they are worthy." Perhaps the true disciples in the city of Sardis had simply remembered and kept their covenants. Speaking to this principle, Elder Carlos E. Asay stated:

> Don't forget that the word *garment* is used symbolically in the scriptures and gives expanded meaning to other words such as *white, clean, pure, righteous, modesty, covering, ceremonial, holy, priesthood, beautiful, perfection, salvation, undefiled, worthy, white raiment, shield, protection, spotless, blameless, armor, covenants, promises, blessings, respect, eternal life*, and so forth. . . .
>
> How wonderful it would be if all Church members walked with God in white and were numbered with the Saints in Sardis![48]

Our efforts to remember the Lord in our lives are always endorsed by the Lord. When we choose to remember the Lord through the righteous use of temple garments, or when we keep a journal or record family moments or organize social media posts to better document family history, these efforts help us to better recognize the hand of the Lord in our lives. To this point, President Henry B. Eyring shared:

> When our children were very small, I started to write down a few things about what happened every day. . . . I never missed a day no matter how tired I was or how early I would have to start the next day. Before I would write, I would ponder this question: "Have I seen the hand of God reaching out to touch us or our children or our family today?" As I kept at it, something began to happen. . . . Testimony grew. I became ever more certain that our Heavenly Father hears and answers prayers. . . .
>
> My point is to urge you to find ways to recognize and remember God's kindness. . . .
>
> Tonight, and tomorrow night, you might pray and ponder, asking the questions: Did God send a message that was just for me? Did I see His hand in my life or the lives of my children? I will do that. And then I will find a way to

---

48 Carlos E. Asay, "The Temple Garment: An Outward Expression of an Inward Commitment," *Ensign*, Sept. 1999.

preserve that memory for the day . . . I testify that He loves us and blesses us, more than most of us have yet recognized.[49]

The Lord's lessons to the Sardis saints are meant for us as well. May we always remember Him!

## AN APPLICATION

*How well do you remember and record the Lord's dealings with you throughout each day? Do you keep a journal or a family history?*

## TO THE CHURCH IN PHILADELPHIA (REV. 3:7–13)

The church in Philadelphia is unique among the seven churches, because it is the only church against whom the Lord registers no complaint.[50] Because of their worthiness, these saints had communion with the Lord and were not shut out or separated from Him. It is important to remember that no one can close that door between us and the Savior but us, ourselves. Sister Chieko N. Okazaki shared:

> Usually when someone says, "I know your works. I know what you're doing," don't we usually think, "Oh, no! You know what I'm *doing?*" and begin to feel guilty or self-conscious! . . . [Revelation 3:8 reads,] "I know thy works: behold, I have set before thee an open door." . . . Isn't there a feeling of triumph in what he's saying? He sets before us an open door that we are completely free to walk in and out of, as we choose. No one can close that door between us and the Savior.[51]

A meteorologist predicts weather based on data and historical records; he or she does not *cause* the weather to happen. The Lord works much the same way (but with much better data!). His foresight does not force us to do things, nor does it constrict our agency. We should not blame

49 Henry B. Eyring, "O Remember, Remember," *Ensign*, Nov. 2007.
50 The historic American city of Philadelphia, Pennsylvania, is named for the church in Rev. 3:7–13. The biblical city of Philadelphia was located about 28 miles southeast of the city of Sardis and was the youngest of the seven cities whose churches John the Revelator addressed in these seven letters. Philadelphia was founded around 150 B.C. by King Attalus of Pergamos, who was noted for the admiration and love he had for his brother, Eumenes, after whom he named this city.
51 Chieko N. Okazaki, *Lighten Up!* (Salt Lake City: Deseret Book, 1993), 169–70.

the weatherman for his forecast or for the weather, just as we should not assign blame to God for what happens in our lives. Rather, we should trust that His omniscience will bring peace and comfort, knowing His meteorological charts are valid and purposeful.

What did the Lord observe with the Saints in Philadelphia? We read in Revelation 3:10, "Because thou hast kept the word of my patience, I also will keep thee from the hour of temptation, which shall come upon all the world, to try them that dwell upon the earth." Patience, in this verse, refers to being steadfast and constant.[52] This type of patience is characteristic of people who are faithful despite opposition. Patience, then, is simply the ability to endure opposition or suffering with faith in God's purposes and timing. Saints today should strive to develop patience by seeking to do God's will and accepting His timing, trusting that He will fulfill all of His promises. As we learn to be patient in small things, we prepare ourselves to face larger trials with that same patience. Alma, in the Book of Mormon, helps us understand patience:

37. [A]s the tree beginneth to grow . . . if ye nourish it with much care it will get root, and grow up, and bring forth fruit.
42. And because of your diligence and your faith and your patience . . . ye shall pluck the fruit thereof, which is most precious, which is sweet above all that is sweet . . .
43. Then . . . ye shall reap the rewards of your faith, and your diligence, and patience. (Alma 32:37, 42–43)

Impatience, on the other hand, is a symptom of selfishness and self-absorption. President Dieter F. Uchtdorf taught:

We live in a world offering fast food, instant messaging, on-demand movies, and immediate answers to the most trivial or profound questions. We don't like to wait. . . .

Patience—the ability to put our desires on hold for a time—is a precious and rare virtue. . . .

Nevertheless, without patience, we cannot please God; we cannot become perfect. Indeed, patience is a purifying

---

52 "Hupomoné" (5281). In *Strong's Concordance*, accessed June 19, 2017, biblehub. com/greek/1404.htm. Here, the Greek word for patience is defined as "cheerful endurance."

process that refines understanding, deepens happiness, focuses action, and offers hope for peace. . . . Our Heavenly Father knows what good parents come to understand over time: if children are ever going to mature and reach their potential, they must learn to wait.[53]

The Lord's message through John to the believers in Philadelphia is vibrant: let us be patient with others and with the Lord.

## AN APPLICATION
*How is your level of patience with events in your life?*

### TO THE CHURCH IN LAODICEA (REV. 3:14–22)
Through a complex system of aqueducts, water was piped to Laodicea from two cities. Hierapolis, to the north, was home to a hot spring, and, to the south, the city of Colossae enjoyed the refreshingly cool waters of the Lycus River. But by the time the waters of these two rivers reached the Laodiceans, it was anything but refreshing. It became tepid and calcified or, quoting from Revelation 3:16, *lukewarm*. Revelation 3:15–16 reads, "I know thy works, that thou art neither cold nor hot: I would thou were cold or hot. So then because thou art lukewarm, and neither cold nor hot, I will spue thee out of my mouth."

Like the church at Sardis, Laodicea may have been bitten by the bug of complacency. Revelation 3:17 tells us that what drove people to be lukewarm was their self-sufficiency: "Because thou sayest, I am rich, and increased with goods, and have need of nothing; and knowest not that thou art wretched, and miserable, and poor, and blind, and naked." The problem with the Laodicean church appears to be that its members lived a life of spiritual apathy. Many times, we too, if we are honest, live that way. Sometimes we live as if we can take care of ourselves, forgetting our dependence on Christ, which can lead us to living as lukewarm disciples.

The Lord can't do too much with us if we're lukewarm or striving for independence from God. He wants us to choose Him (see Matt. 6:24). To that, President Marion G. Romney taught, "Now there are [those among us] who [are trying] to serve the Lord without offending the devil."[54] Sterling W. Sill similarly taught:

---

53 Dieter F. Uchtdorf, "Continue in Patience," *Ensign*, May 2010.
54 Marion G. Romney, "The Prince of Peace," *Ensign*, Oct. 1983.

[B]y holding back in our faith, we become holdouts on God and members of the unfortunate group that someone called "life's half-believers." They are those who believe just a part of the time, or they believe in just some of the [doctrines]. This makes us guilty of those great sins of fractional devotion and marginal morals, which produces a minimal performance. . . . Then much of the time we remain as if we were wallowing in the slime of the low tide. We are left straddling the fence, and our dim understanding leaves us uncertain as to which way we should go.[55]

Conversion and salvation do not come by half commitment. We are expected to give our *all*, not just a part. We cannot survive spiritually with one foot in the Church and the other in the world. We must make the choice. Faith is belief that is put into action.[56] This definition of faith is the difference between our asking if someone has a pilot's license and having faith enough in that person's qualifications to actually get into the plane and let the pilot fly it.

What was the cause of the apparent halfhearted commitment of the saints in Laodicea? John wrote in Revelation 3:17, "[T]hou sayest, I am rich, and increased with goods, and have need of nothing." Perhaps the sin of greed had caused these believers to split their loyalty. Saul, in the book of Proverbs, wrote that "he that maketh haste to be rich shall not be innocent" (Prov. 28:20). Simply stated, the more we have, the more we want.

President Spencer W. Kimball asked:

Why another of anything if one has that already which provides the necessities and reasonable luxuries? Why continue to expand and increase holdings, especially when those increased responsibilities draw one's interests away from proper family and spiritual commitments, and from those things to which the Lord would have us give precedence in our lives? Why must we always be

---

55 Sterling W. Sill, *Principles, Promises, and Powers* (Salt Lake City: Deseret Book, 1973), 137–38.
56 "Gospel Topics: Faith in Jesus Christ," *The Church of Jesus Christ of Latter-day Saints*, accessed Jun. 6, 2017, https://www.lds.org.

expanding to the point where our interests are divided and our attentions and thoughts are upon the things of the world? Certainly when one's temporal possessions become great, it is very difficult for one to give proper attention to the spiritual things.[57]

Elder Joe J. Christensen gives three simple suggestions that help us gauge our view and feelings about money: "[Do] not confuse wants with needs," "live modestly and avoid debt," and "be generous in giving . . . [to] others."[58] Our greed begins when we think more about what God owes us than what we owe Him. Remember, the Lord has promised the faithful "the riches of eternity" (D&C 38:39). Let us avoid the laziness and lukewarm temperatures in our modern-day Laodicea.

## AN APPLICATION

*How dependent on God are you for your needs? Do you find yourself seeking to obtain more and more things? Are you truly grateful and content with what you've been given?*

Suffice it to say that Revelation 2–3 gives us hope in Jesus Christ. Despite our shortcomings and follies, we can indeed overcome through hearkening to divine chastening. This foundational principle is a blessing, as it anchors us to Christ and His Atonement as we continue to study about and prepare for His return.

---

57 Spencer W. Kimball, "Keep Your Money Clean," *Conference Report*, Oct. 1953, 54–55.
58 Joe J. Christensen, "Greed, Selfishness, and Overindulgence," *Ensign*, May 1999.

# *Revelation 4–5*
## VISIONS OF HEAVEN

RECALL FROM OUR OUTLINE IN Revelation 1:19 that Revelation 4 marks a transition in the book. In Revelation 4, John has a vision of heaven wherein he receives his call prior to the events of Revelation 5, in which Christ opens the seven seals.[59, 60] The Savior invites John, "Come up hither, and I will shew thee things which must be hereafter" (Rev. 4:1), and John divulges: "And Immediately I was in the spirit: and, behold, a throne was set in heaven, and one sat on the throne" (Rev. 4:2). John saw twenty-four elders surrounding the throne (Rev. 4:4) and also "four beasts full of eyes before and behind. And the first beast was like a lion, and the second beast like a calf, and the third beast had a face as a man, and the fourth beast was like a flying eagle" (Rev. 4:6–8).

---

59 Rev. 4:6 describes the world that John saw as "a sea of glass." Modern revelation teaches that "[the earth will] be one great urim and thummim, and the Saints [will be able to] look in it and see as they are seen" (Joseph Smith, *History of the Church* 5:279). President Brigham Young further added, "This earth will become a celestial body—be like a sea of glass, or like a urim and thummim; and when you wish to know anything, you can look in this earth and see all the eternities of God" (*Journal of Discourses* 8:200).

60 Orson Pratt taught, "There are many things we cannot feel, yet we have knowledge of them . . . when this spirit is freed from this mortal tabernacle . . . all these senses will be greatly enlarged. If we, by looking through these little eyes of ours, can see objects some thousands of millions of miles distant . . . Then unclothe the spirit and instead of exposing a small portion . . . the whole of it would be exposed. I think we could then see in different directions at once, instead of looking in one particular direction; we could then look all around us at the same instant" (*Journal of Discourses* 2:244). Joseph Smith reported after seeing the vision of the three degrees of glory (D&C 76), "My whole body was full of light and I could see even out at the ends of my fingers and toes" (Nels B. Lundwall, *The Vision or The Degrees of Glory* [Salt Lake City: Deseret Book 2008], 11).

Joseph Smith inquired of the Lord to know the nature of the beasts in Revelation 4 and 5, and he received Doctrine and Covenants 77 in response. The Lord told Joseph that the beasts are exalted creatures from other worlds representing the four classes of animals on our planet (see D&C 77:3). The four beasts were identified as being the highest, or most powerful, beasts of their kind—the lion among wild animals, the calf among domesticated animals, the eagle among the birds, and man among all living things.

Joseph Fielding Smith further clarified,

> We are to understand that there will be beasts of various kinds, after the resurrection, in each of the kingdoms, telestial, terrestrial, and celestial. It would be a very strange thing for any of the kingdoms to be devoid of animal and plant life. . . . They are the creations of the Almighty . . . according to the divine plan, [He will] make all of his creatures as happy as it is possible for them to be under the conditions of their immortal states.[61]

Let's look at some details in this chapter and seek personal application. Notice that these beasts and the twenty-four elders that surround the throne of God "cast their crowns before the throne, saying, Thou art worthy, O Lord, to receive glory and honour and power: for thou hast created all things, and for thy pleasure they are and were created" (Rev. 4:10–11). Crowns are a symbol of power and control and dominion,[62] but they can also be interpreted as abilities and gifts from our Heavenly Father.[63] Notice here that these worshippers are quick to surrender their crowns to God the Father, giving Him the glory. Elder Bruce R. McConkie revealed:

> Those who gain exaltation in the highest heaven of the celestial world shall wear crowns. Perhaps literal crowns may be worn on occasion—emblematic of their victory over the world and signifying that they rule and reign as kings and queens in the eternal house of Israel. . . . There is and always will be only one King over Israel, Christ Jesus. The crowns will be thrown back to Him signifying the devotion to our King.[64]

61 Joseph Fielding Smith, *Church History and Modern Revelation*, 2:68.
62 See D&C 20:14, Moses 7:56, Joseph Smith—Matthew 1:1.
63 See Larry Hiller, "A Crown of Thorns, a Crown of Glory," *Ensign* Apr. 2011.
64 Bruce R. McConkie, "Crowns," *Mormon Doctrine* (Salt Lake City: Deseret Book, 1966), 124.

What *crowns* are we given from the Lord here on Earth? They could be crowns of talent or abilities, crowns of influence, or crowns of finances. Do you, for example, wear a crown of popularity, or a crown of creativity or fashion or intellect? A crown of having a beautiful family or successful children? These are all worthy crowns from our King. Orson Pratt asked:

> [W]hat are we to understand by this crown of righteousness, which is to be given to the Saints? We understand that it is actually to be a crown of glory; that they are to be kings in reality. . . . Compared with this, what are all the little, petty kingdoms of this earth worth? They are not worth one snap of the finger . . . [We] will be like Gods, and will hold dominion under that Being who is the Lord of lords; and [we] will hold it to all eternity.[65]

Accordingly, we should beware of any false crowns that we could be tempted to place above the righteous crowns God offers. The crowns of pride, haughtiness, or ego taint the true crowns that the Lord has gifted us.

Recall what the worshippers did with their crowns in Revelation 4:10–11. They took them off and gave them to the One who sat on the throne. With this in mind, what should we do with our crowns? We should be willing to surrender any talent or other crowns and place them at the feet of the Master. The Savior is going to do a lot more with those crowns than we can do on our own.

*Adonai* has become one of my favorite titles for God. It means *owner* or *ruler* and originally dealt with masters who owned slaves. Yet the title *Adonai* didn't merely connote ownership; it also bore within the name a certain responsibility for the care and well-being of that which was owned. The *Adonai* was to provide for, protect, and guide that which he owned. The psalmist pens in Psalms 97:5 that God is "the Lord of the whole earth." Since God is not only the Creator, but also the absolute ruler and owner, our position should be one of surrender and of submissiveness. Submission is a powerful tool when coupled with an all-powerful Adonai. His is the perspective we should utilize in making choices. As we surrender our will and our crowns to our Adonai, the heavens pour out blessings.

While Jesus was on the Sea of Galilee teaching, food became scarce (see Matt. 14:13–21). The disciples began to scramble to find sustenance

---

65 Brigham Young, *Journal of Discourses* (London: F. D. and S. W. Richards, 1854–1886), 1:291.

for the multitude. In John 6:9, we read that a young boy was among the crowd and had with him five loaves and two fishes. His willingness to share helped in this plight. Personally, I can picture this little lad humbly offering his metaphorical crowns by stating, "I've got five loaves and two fishes." If I were one of the disciples, I might have replied, "Okay, nice try, young man. We've got thousands of people and there's no way that five loaves and two fishes can feed this group. You simply don't have enough . . ." But then the Master breaks that little offering and there is enough to feed everyone, including having leftovers!

Notice the pattern: the boy offers his "crown" (his loaves and fishes) and the Lord receives it, blesses it, and then uses it to bless others. The same is true in our lives. As President Ezra Taft Benson taught:

> [M]en and women who turn their lives over to God will discover that He can make a lot more out of their lives than they can. He will deepen their joys, expand their vision, quicken their minds, strengthen their muscles, lift their spirits, multiply their blessings, increase their opportunities, comfort their souls, raise up friends, and pour out peace.[66]

We have been commanded, "Let your light so shine before men, that they may see your good works, and glorify your Father which is in heaven" (Matt. 5:16). Notice what happens to the crowns in Revelation 5:10: these worshippers who once removed their crowns have received their crowns back in return. They have become "kings and priests" who "shall reign on the earth." It appears, by way of application, that as we turn our will over to God, He will make our lives richer, giving our crowns back, but having made them better than we thought possible.

To borrow a principle for application from the Old Testament, in Exodus 1:8–11 we learn that when a new king came to power in Egypt who did not know the great Joseph, he feared because the children of Israel were larger in number than his people. He set taskmasters over them to afflict them with burdens. Exodus 1:12 reads, "But the more they afflicted them, the more they multiplied and grew." What a sweet principle: the more they were afflicted, the more they multiplied. Consider this hypothetical example from the Missional Challenge website: Suppose we had a checkerboard with 64 squares. If on the first square we were to place one grain of wheat and on the second square two grains, and on the third

---

66 Ezra Taft Benson, "Jesus Christ—Gifts and Expectations," *Ensign*, Dec. 1988, 4.

square four grains, and so on, how much wheat would we need to place on the last square if we continued doubling each succeeding square? The answer is astounding: It would take enough wheat to cover India fifty feet deep! The multiplication process is exponential. [67] The Lord can indeed *add* blessings, but He loves to *multiply* blessings even more. You see, once we turn our crowns over to the Master, He will multiply these gifts and, in turn, feed thousands.

**AN APPLICATION**

*How eager are you to give your crowns over to the Lord? How often do you proactively volunteer your time, talents, and possessions to help others?*

Next, we turn to Revelation 5. Here, the Savior opens the book sealed with seven seals (see Rev. 5:1–8) and, in the process, we gain a beautiful insight about the relationship the Savior has with us. Central to His role is His desire for us to have a relationship with Him.

As a father, a good relationship with my children is my highest hope; I do hope that my children make wise choices in their lives, but above that I hope that they seek to have a deep and meaningful relationship with me as their father, knowing that good choices will naturally stem from the loving relationship I share with them. Elder Jeffrey R. Holland taught:

> It is the grand truth that in all that Jesus came to say and do . . . He was showing us who and what God our Eternal Father is like, how completely devoted He is to His children in every age and nation. In word and deed, Jesus was trying to reveal and make personal to us the true nature of His Father, our Father in Heaven.
>
> He did this . . . because then and now all of us need to know God more fully in order to love Him more deeply and obey Him more completely. . . .
>
> So feeding the hungry, healing the sick, rebuking hypocrisy, pleading for faith—this was Christ showing us the way of the Father. [68]

The Lord's throne is surrounded by "ten thousand times ten thousand, and thousands of thousands" (Rev. 5:11), which gives each of us hope that

---

67 "Disciplemaking: Addition verse Multiplication," *Missional Challenge: Live the Mission*, accessed Jun. 7, 2017, https://www.missionalchallenge.com/disciplemaking-addition-vs-multiplication/.
68 Jeffrey R. Holland, "The Grandeur of God," *Ensign,* Nov. 2003.

we will be found among the assembly as well. John continues, "And every creature which is in heaven, and on the earth, and under the earth, and such as are in the sea, and all that are in them, heard I saying, Blessing, and honour, and glory, and power, be unto him that sitteth upon the throne, and unto the Lamb for ever and ever" (Rev. 5:13).

Stephen E. Robinson, a Latter-day Saint author, shared an experience he had as a bishop that illustrates the principle of hope found in Revelation 5. He recalled:

> I once counseled a man who said, "Bishop, I'm just not celestial material." Well, I'd heard those words once too often, so I said, "You're not celestial material? Welcome to the club. Not one of us is! Not one of us qualifies on our own for the presence of God. So why don't you admit your real problem? Why don't you admit that you don't believe Christ can do what he says he can do?"
>
> He got angry. "I have a testimony of Jesus!"
>
> I said, "Yes, you believe in Christ. You simply do not *believe* Christ. He says that even though you are not celestial, he can make you celestial—but you don't believe it." . . .
>
> There is no other way. Many of us are trying to save ourselves, holding the atonement of Jesus Christ at arm's distance and saying, "When I've perfected myself, then I'll be worthy of the Atonement." But that's not how it works. That's like saying, "I won't take the medicine until I'm well. I'll be worthy of it then."[69]

Every year, seminary and institute teachers receive training from one of the General Authorities, and quite often an Apostle is chosen to teach. One particular year, Elder Bruce R. McConkie was the speaker. He reportedly asked the group of seminary and institute instructors present which kingdom, in their opinion, would be the largest. In other words, at the very close of the latter days, after the final judgement, when all is said and done, which kingdom will house the most people? There was some discussion, and he asked this group of teachers to vote. He asked them to raise their hands if they thought the telestial kingdom will be the most

---

69 Stephen E. Robinson, "Believing Christ," *Ensign*, Apr. 1992.

populated. A few hands went up. When he asked them who thought the terrestrial will have the most souls, some more hands went up. He then asked who felt that the celestial kingdom will have the largest number of people, and a few hands went up. At this response, Elder McConkie reportedly said, "How dare you think that Satan will win and Christ will lose?" Then he continued. "[God's] work and [His] glory [is to] bring to pass the immortality and eternal life of man" (see Moses 1:39), and He's good at what He does."[70]

I love that declaration! The Savior is on our team; He is rooting for us and working to save us and our families, and the number of people who have achieved the celestial kingdom as seen in Revelation 5 should give us hope that we may qualify for that reward. However, many Latter-day Saints wonder if they are even capable of reaching the celestial kingdom. BYU professor Alonzo L. Gaskill taught in his book *Odds Are You're Going to Be Exalted* that we often misunderstand the plan of happiness and the Lord's actual requirements for us; this in turn leads to self-doubt. Brother Gaskill takes into account God's mercy, the power of the Atonement of Jesus Christ, the opportunity to repent in the spirit world, and the purification in the Millennium, concluding that exaltation may not only be possible but is statistically probable.

Joseph Smith reminded us, "It is the first principle of the gospel to know for a certainty the character of God,"[71] and this vision of the Lord in Revelation 5 reminds us of this truth: The Lord is full of grace and mercy and compassion. *Grace* is a term that has been beautifully clarified by Brad Wilcox, in his 2011 BYU devotional address. He explained that grace "is not the light at the end of the tunnel but the light that moves us through the tunnel." Grace doesn't help us earn a place in heaven; Grace helps us learn of heaven. "Grace is not about filling gaps," said Wilcox. "[Grace is] about filling us." Grace doesn't just save us from sin; Grace saves us for heaven. The Savior's Atonement isn't just a favor Christ has given to us. Said Omar Canals, a friend of Wilcox's, "it is an investment He made in us." The Atonement of Christ doesn't just cleanse us; it transforms us through grace. Grace does not just allow us to go home to heaven; Grace helps us feel at home when we reach heaven. "Jesus doesn't make *up* the difference. Jesus

---

70 Account from personal witnesses (colleagues of the author) in attendance at a seminary and institute instructor training seminar, BYU campus, Aug. 1983.

71 *Teachings of the Prophet Joseph Smith*, compiled by Joseph Fielding Smith (Salt Lake City: Deseret Book, 1977), 345.

makes *all* the difference . . . [Grace] is not a finishing touch; [Grace] is the Finisher's touch."[72] President J. Reuben Clark, Jr. testified:

> You know, I believe that the Lord will help us . . . I believe that our Heavenly Father wants to save every one of his children. I do not think he intends to shut any of us off because of some slight transgression, some slight failure to observe some rule or regulation. There are the great elementals that we must observe, but he is not going to be captious about the lesser things. . . .
>
> I believe that in his justice and mercy, he will give us the maximum reward for our acts, give us all that he can give, and in the reverse, I believe that he will impose upon us the minimum penalty which it is possible for him to impose.[73]

Recall from Exodus 4:10 that Moses was "of a slow tongue." Enoch was slow of speech, and everyone hated him (Moses 6:31). Paul had a "thorn in the flesh" that he asked God to remove three times and it never was removed (2 Cor. 12:7–9). By way of application, if God hasn't removed the *it* from your life, *it* is not a mistake. God showed Moses that He had all power by causing Moses's hand to become leprous and then healing it (Ex. 4:6–7); certainly the Lord could have easily shown Moses His power by replacing his tongue with one a bit more fluid, but He didn't. Why? Well, as the scriptures say, "[His] grace is sufficient" (2 Cor. 12:9). What He offers is *enough*. It's more than adequate; His grace is ample and plentiful. I am grateful that John was a witness to this truth of God's saving grace, evident in Revelation 5!

### AN APPLICATION

*Do you have a testimony of God? Is your view of the Godhead and Their characters accurate? Does it reflect what prophets have taught about the nature of the Godhead? Do you believe in Christ—and also believe Christ?*

---

72 Brad Wilcox, "His Grace is Sufficient," *Ensign*, Sept. 2013; Brad Wilcox, "His Grace is Sufficient," *BYU Speeches*, accessed Jun. 7, 2017, https://speeches.byu.edu/talks/brad-wilcox_his-grace-is-sufficient/.

73 J. Reuben Clark, Jr. in *Conference Report*, Sept. 30, 1955, 24.

## *Revelation 6*
## AN OVERVIEW OF THE SEVEN SEALS

IN REVELATION 6, JOHN SAW the history of Earth's existence. Of this panoramic vision, Joseph Smith inquired of the Lord and received the following revelation from the Doctrine and Covenants in response:

> 6. Q. What are we to understand by the book which John saw, which was sealed on the back with seven seals?
> A. We are to understand that it contains the revealed will, mysteries, and the works of God; the hidden things of his economy concerning this earth during the seven thousand years of its continuance, or its temporal existence.
> 7. Q. What are we to understand by the seven seals with which it was sealed?
> A. We are to understand that the first seal contains the things of the first thousand years, and the second also of the second thousand years, and so on until the seventh. (D&C 77:6–7)

In his 1987 talk, Elder Gerald N. Lund pointed out that John's vision of Earth's history in the book of Revelation is 317 verses in length and yet he spends only eleven verses (about 3.5 percent) on the first five thousand years of Earth's history. In Revelation 20, the Millennium is discussed in only seven verses (about 2.2 percent of the entire book). Elder Lund said, "By far the largest portion of the book [well over 75 percent] describes the events that immediately precede the Second Coming of the Savior."[74]

The seven thousand years of the Earth's existence are divided as follows:

---

74 Gerald N. Lund, "Seeing the Book of Revelation As a Book of Revelation," *Ensign*, Dec. 1987.

First Seal: Revelation 6:1–2 (about 4000 B.C. to 3000 B.C.)
- John saw a warrior on a white horse, conquering, symbolic of Adam and Enoch and Zion.

Second Seal: Revelation 6:3–4 (about 3000 B.C. to 2000 B.C.)
- John saw a representation of death on a red horse, symbolic of violence, wickedness, and the great Flood.

Third Seal: Revelation 6:5–6 (about 2000 B.C. to 1000 B.C.)
- John saw images of famine on a black horse, symbolic of the days of Abraham and Joseph.

Fourth Seal: Revelation 6:7–8 (about 1000 B.C. to A.D. 1)
- John saw a pale rider, symbolizing death by war, famine, and beasts, along with empires and conquering nations, symbolic of the intertestamental period and the days of Alexander the Great.

Fifth Seal: Revelation 6:9–11 (about A.D. 1 to A.D. 1000)
- John saw the martyrs for Christ of the early Christian era.

Sixth Seal: Revelation 6:12–7:17 (about A.D. 1000 to A.D. 2000)
- John saw natural disasters as signs of the last days, the Restoration of the gospel, and temple blessings.

Seventh Seal: Revelation 8:1 onward.
- John prophesied of two prophets killed in Jerusalem, Christ's appearance at the Mount of Olives, the battle of Armageddon, the destruction of Satan's kingdom, and Christ's appearance to the world.

Natural disasters continue, Babylon is destroyed, Jesus Christ comes in glory, Satan is bound, the righteous join the Savior in the clouds, peace reigns for a millennium, Satan is loosed for a season, the last great battle is fought; final judgment occurs, and Earth receives its celestial glory.

**THE FIRST SEAL**

The four horsemen appear in Revelation 6 and are symbols of the first 4000 years of the Earth's existence. The first horseman, found in Revelation 6:2 and representing the first 1000 years of Earth's existence, is riding a white horse. White is a symbol of purity, typifying the days of Adam and Enoch. Certainly the level of purity of Adam and Eve, and also those under Enoch's leadership, was remarkable. As Elder M. Russell Ballard taught, "[P]urity precedes power,"[75] and we each gain strength and power through faith in

75 M. Russell Ballard, "Purity Precedes Power," *Ensign*, Nov. 1990.

Jesus Christ and His Atonement. The Lord, throughout scripture, has listed several principles of purity to help us gain power:

- "He that hath clean hands, and a pure heart . . . shall receive the [Lord's blessings]" (Ps. 24:3–5).
- "[B]e ye clean, that bear the vessels of the Lord" (Isa. 52:11).
- "Blessed are the pure in heart" (Matt. 5:8).
- "[W]hatsoever things are pure . . . think on these things" (Philip. 4:8).
- "[B]e purified even as [Christ] is pure" (Moro. 7:48).
- Christ will reserve unto himself a pure people (D&C 43:14).
- The pure shall see God (D&C 97:10–17).
- "[T]his is Zion—the pure in heart" (D&C 97:21).

For an application, let's look back to the thirteenth century. Explorers and seafaring Crusaders frequently suffered from a condition called scurvy. Its symptoms included fatigue, spots on the skin, spongy gums, depression, open wounds, loss of teeth, fever, and finally death from bleeding.[76] It had been estimated that scurvy caused the death of at least two million sailors between 1500 and 1800.[77] However, the prevention of scurvy is simple: citrus fruit. There is one vitamin that is lacking that causes the development of scurvy: vitamin C. Sometimes people suffer painful consequences because they lack one simple nutrient: the purifying effect of the gospel of Jesus Christ, our vitamin *J*.

**AN APPLICATION**

*How would you rate the level of purity in your life?*

**THE SECOND SEAL**

In Revelation 6:4, a red horse appears next, symbolizing violence and typifying the days of Noah. In the Pearl of Great Price we read that "the earth was corrupt before God, and it was filled with violence" (Moses 8:28). During Noah's ministry in the second thousand years of Earth's existence, all but eight souls were destroyed in the Flood.

It appears that this horseman was a soldier in Satan's army who championed violence among the children of men. Why had Earth become such a violent place? In part, it was because the rider of the blood-red

---

76 "Scurvy," *Dictionary.com*, accessed Jun. 7, 2017, www.dictionary.com
77 "Scurvy," *Wikipedia*, accessed Jun. 7, 2017, https://en.wikipedia.org/wiki/Scurvy.

horse described in Revelation 6 was given power, "to take peace from the earth . . . that they should kill one another" (Rev. 6:4).

Looking for relevancy in this principle to our lives, the *For the Strength of Youth* pamphlet counsels:

> Do not attend, view, or participate in anything that is vulgar, immoral, violent, or pornographic in any way. Do not participate in anything that presents immorality or violence as acceptable. Have the courage to walk out of a movie, change your music, or turn off a computer, television, or mobile device if what you see or hear drives away the Spirit.[78]

Toll roads provide a good analogy of this principle of Satan's snares. Toll roads are common in most major cities. Drivers can enter these roads for free, typically travel at a faster speed with less traffic, but each driver must pay a toll at the end of the ride. In application, many people enter lifestyles or make choices that seem free at first; they enter a toll road and begin driving at a faster speed and with less traffic, smiling as they speed to their destination. But a toll road is not a freeway: there is a price that must be paid when it's time to exit. The toll roads of pornography or immorality or dishonesty may look much like freeways, but they are toll roads with prices to be paid at some point during the drive. Indeed, one principle for application we can discern from the second horseman in Revelation 6 is that of the importance of remaining pure and avoiding the tempting toll roads life offers.

### AN APPLICATION

*Are you free from media that shows violent imagery or other inappropriate content? Are you currently on a toll road or a freeway in your life?*

### THE THIRD SEAL

In Revelation 6:5 the third horseman, who appears during the earth's third thousand years, is riding a black horse. Black is symbolic of death and starvation. During the third thousand years of Earth's existence, as the prophets continued to teach, people were scattered and separated. The city of Salem, ruled by Melchizedek, was righteous and powerful,

---

78 "Entertainment." In *For the Strength of Youth* (Salt Lake City: The Church of Jesus Christ of Latter-day Saints, 2011), 11.

but it was in stark contrast to the city of Babel and the people's wicked desire to enter heaven independent of the Atonement of Jesus Christ. Years after being scattered due to the confounding of language, a covenant people emerged and Israel became the center from which God's law was delivered. These days of Abraham, Isaac, Jacob, and Joseph were filled with starvation and drought and death during the third thousand years.

In our day, Heavenly Father has commanded us to "prepare every needful thing" (D&C 109:8) so that, should adversity come, we may care for ourselves and our neighbors and support bishops as they care for others.

The First Presidency has counseled:

> We encourage Church members worldwide to prepare for adversity in life by having a basic supply of food and water and some money in savings.
>
> We ask that you be wise as you store food and water and build your savings. Do not go to extremes; it is not prudent, for example, to go into debt to establish your food storage all at once. With careful planning, you can, over time, establish a home storage supply and a financial reserve.[79]

Do you have a three-month supply of food and water? One way to do this is to purchase a few extra items each week and add it to your food storage. Then you can gradually increase your supply until it is sufficient for three months. How is your long-term food supply? Continue gradually building your supply until you have enough to sustain you in the event of longer periods of famine or difficulty. Do you have adequate drinking water storage? Store water in sturdy, leak-proof, break-resistant containers. Consider using plastic bottles commonly used for juices and soda. How is your financial reserve? Establish a financial reserve by saving a little money each week and gradually increasing it to a reasonable amount. These are great principles gleaned from the third horseman in Revelation 6.

### AN APPLICATION

*How would you rate your level of temporal preparedness for the Second Coming?*

---

79 *All Is Safely Gathered In: Family Home Storage* pamphlet (IRI, 2007).

## THE FOURTH SEAL

The fourth and final horse was pale and had two riders: death and hell (physical death and spiritual death). During the fourth thousand year period, vicious generals and armies waged terrible wars. Some of the world's greatest empires came to power and also fell, including Babylon, Assyria, Persia, Macedonia, and others. Prophets such as Hosea, Amos, Isaiah, and later Jeremiah and Lehi tried to warn followers of the pending doom, but few heeded their message.

The pale horse represents the appearance of the face of the dead. The spiritually dead are pale because their countenance lacks the Light of Christ. The word *countenance* refers to the way a person's face expresses his or her character. Book of Mormon prophet Alma poignantly asked, "Have ye received his image in your countenance?" (Alma 5:14). And 2 Corinthians 3:18 tells us, "But we all, with open face beholding as in a glass the glory of the Lord, are changed into the same image from glory to glory, even as by the Spirit of the Lord." As the Spirit of the Lord works within us, we can become more and more like Him and mirror or reflect His love and glory.

How do we get the Light of Christ to shine brightly in our lives? Revelation 5:8 tells us that the four beasts and four and twenty elders were carrying "golden vials full of odours, which are the prayers of Saints." It appears that our daily prayers aren't fleeting. They don't just disappear. Rather, our prayers are placed (maybe symbolically) in golden vials to be treasured in heaven.

Interestingly, while on the earth, Jesus's disciples did not ask too many doctrinal questions of the Savior. Among the questions they did ask in the scriptures was: Will you teach us how to pray? (see Luke 11). Among all of the things the disciples wanted to know from Jesus, they were interested in praying as He prayed. Why? They must have sensed a deep relationship between Christ and His Father, and the disciples wanted that divine intimacy as well.[80]

In the following scriptures and several other times in the Doctrine and Covenants, very similar to the principle in Revelation 6, the Lord

80 Relationships are central to the gospel and are key to faith in Jesus Christ. Faith-based relationships, then, require a "not my will, but thine, be done" (Luke 22:42) approach to God. When people have a good relationship with God the Father (gained through prayer, study, and obedience) but answers don't come or they contradict the request, there is no loss of faith because there is no loss in the relationship. Gaining that type of closeness with God occurs largely in private prayer.

reminds us of His attentiveness to our prayers. "[Y]our prayers have entered into the ears of the Lord of Sabaoth, and are recorded with this seal and testament" (D&C 98:2), and "the alms of your prayers have come up into the ears of the Lord of Sabaoth, and are recorded in the book of the names of the sanctified" (D&C 88:2). Prayer is spiritual work that should ideally be preceded by preparation.[81] Scheduling sufficient time to communicate with Heavenly Father the deepest desires of our hearts is key and helps us invite the Holy Ghost to guide us in knowing what to pray for.

Rarely do we see personal prayer modeled. When we attend church, classes, firesides, or other meetings (including family prayer or when we pray as a married couple), we hear and participate in public prayer. Consequently, our personal prayer patterns may reflect the public prayer model. Below are two tables, one delineating common doctrines and practices that should accompany *all* prayers, and the other delineating key differences between public and private prayer.[82, 83, 84, 85]

| DOCTRINES AND PRACTICES FOR ALL PRAYER |
| --- |
| God hears and answers all prayers (1 John 5:14). |
| We should follow the proper pattern of prayer and use of reverent pronouns.[82] |
| Seeking for and being inspired by the Holy Ghost before and as we pray should be paramount.[83] |
| We should express gratitude as we pray.[84] |
| We should always pray with real intent and without vain repetition (3 Ne. 13:4; Moro. 10:3–5). |
| The purpose of prayer is to align our will with God's.[85] |
| We should be eager to "go and do" at the conclusion of prayer (1 Ne. 3:7, 4:6). |

---

81 Prayer is much more than a *pretty please* to the Lord (just as fasting is not a hunger strike). As we approach our Lord through prayer, fasting, or scripture study, our hopes should include being filled with the Holy Ghost, learning God's will, and ultimately aligning our will with His. Christ is the Son of Righteousness, implying that one title for God is *Righteousness*. As we hunger and thirst after righteousness, we really are seeking God's will and becoming more like Him. Truly seeking for and establishing a relationship with Deity requires time spent in prayer, study, and fasting.

82 See *The Improvement Era* (Salt Lake City: The Church of Jesus Christ of Latter-day Saints, Jun. 1963), 531.

83 See David A. Bednar, "Pray Always," *Ensign*, Nov. 2008.

84 See Christie Skrinak, "Prayer of Gratitude," *Ensign*, Sept. 2013.

85 See Kevin Pearson, "The Power of Personal Prayer." In Devotional talk given at Brigham Young University–Hawaii May 17, 2011.

In addition to containing the elements outlined above, public and private prayers should include specific elements appropriate for their setting, as illustrated in the table below.

| | PUBLIC PRAYER | PERSONAL PRAYER |
|---|---|---|
| **FREQUENCY** | When called upon | "Pray always" |
| **PAUSES** | Short pauses, seeking inspiration | Longer pauses as we listen for answers |
| **DURATION** | Concise | No time limit |
| **FOCUS** | On the meeting | On personal desires, questions, problems, or confessions |
| **REPRESENTING** | Representing others | Representing oneself |
| **PURPOSE** | Unity | Building relationship with Deity |

Personal prayer should be very different from public prayer in its form and purpose. As mentioned previously, people often approach personal prayer using techniques they have seen modeled in public prayer. That is, when engaging in personal prayer, they only pause occasionally, keep their prayer concise, and pray in general terms, each behavior having been appropriately modeled in public prayers. Our personal prayers should occur often and throughout each day and should include confessions, repentance, and longer pauses as we listen and seek to build a relationship with our Heavenly Father. Personal prayer should be time spent enjoying His presence through the Holy Ghost and seeking to align our will with His.[86]

This counsel from Elder M. Russell Ballard is instructive:

> In your morning prayer each new day, ask Heavenly Father to guide you to recognize an opportunity to serve one of His precious children. Then go throughout the

---

[86] To use an analogy from our home, my electrical power strip in my bedroom runs our phone, TV, computer, monitors, printer, and speakers; we've taken a single source of power and, through the use of the power strip, provided power to several devices. Prayer is much like a power strip: when we take desires to the Source (our Heavenly Father), we tap into His power; through Him, we have power to help friends, power to improve our health, power to succeed at work or at school, power within our family, and power in our marriages.

day with your heart full of faith and love, looking for someone to help. Stay focused . . . If you do this, your spiritual sensitivities will be enlarged and you will discover opportunities to serve that you never before realized were possible.[87]

Then, at the end of our day, Elder David A. Bednar counsels that we "report back to our Father. We review the events of the day and express heartfelt thanks for the blessings and the help we received. We repent and . . . identify ways we can do and become better tomorrow."[88] Let us never become pale like the people depicted in the days of the fourth horseman!

## AN APPLICATION

*How are your personal prayers? Do you pray each morning before your day begins and kneel each night to pray again?*

## THE FIFTH SEAL

In Revelation 6, John introduces us to the fifth seal; he saw the early Christian martyrs who suffered death because of their belief in Jesus Christ:

9. And when he had opened the fifth seal, I saw under the altar the souls of them that were slain for the word of God, and for the testimony which they held. . . .
11. And white robes were given unto every one of them; and it was said unto them, that they should rest yet for a little season, until their fellowservants also and their brethren, that should be killed as they were, should be fulfilled. (Rev. 6:9–11)

Doctrine and Covenants counsels us, "Let no man be afraid to lay down his life for my sake; for whoso layeth down his life for my sake shall find it again. And whoso is not willing to lay down his life for my sake is not my disciple" (D&C 103:27–28). In Matthew 22:36–40 one of the Pharisees and the Savior have a discussion about which commandments are the more important, as follows: "Master, which is the great commandment in the law? Jesus said unto him, Thou shalt love the Lord thy God with all thy heart, and with all thy soul, and with all thy mind.

87 M. Russell Ballard, "Be Anxiously Engaged," *Ensign*, Nov. 2012.
88 David A. Bednar, "Pray Always," *Ensign*, Nov. 2008.

This is the first and great commandment. And the second is like unto it, Thou shalt love thy neighbour as thyself. On these two commandments hang all the law and the prophets." Each story in "the law" (the first 5 books of Moses) and every account from the prophets (Joshua through Malachi) are in the Bible to demonstrate to us God's love for us and how we are supposed to love one another.

Jesus Christ said, "Greater love hath no man than this, that a man lay down his life for his friends" (John 15:13). This doesn't mean we have to die to show our love for our friends. We lay down our lives every time we put someone else's needs before our own; we lay down our lives through service. We can do small acts of kindness for our neighbors, take part in community service, fulfill responsibilities within our ward, or contribute to the Church's large-scale humanitarian efforts. These actions and others, whether great or small, let us feel the happiness of connecting with our brothers and sisters while reminding us that God often allows us to be the answer to someone else's prayers.

Those early Christians who were killed for the cause of Christ truly are remarkable men and women of God. Stephen, for example, was stoned to death for his testimony of the Savior (see Acts 7:55–60). Peter was crucified, head down, in Rome; Andrew was burned to death; James was killed by the sword (Acts 12:1–2); Philip was crucified; Bartholomew was beaten, crucified, and then beheaded; Thomas was run through by a lance; Matthew was slain by the sword; James was thrown from a pinnacle and then beaten to death; Thaddæus was shot to death by arrows; Simon was crucified; Judas Iscariot committed suicide by hanging himself (Joseph Smith Translation, Matthew 27:6, Acts 1:18).[89]

What message can we take from the valiancy of those early disciples? We are challenged in 2 Timothy 4:5 to "do the work of an *evangelist*" (emphasis added). Paul the Apostle borrowed the noun *evangel* from the Greek. *Evangel* means *to announce the good news*. During wartimes, a runner (the carrier of the good news—the *evangelist*) would enter the presence of the king or ruler and announce a military victory. When Rome ruled the world and a battle was won, the Roman general would send a runner from the battlefield to the ruler of the Roman Empire. Upon arrival, the runner would kneel at the leader's feet, unroll a scroll, and announce the good news.

Like that band of early believers, we are to *evangelize*, or announce the good news of the Gospel of Jesus Christ and his victory!

---

89 Shanna Butler, "What Happened to Christ's Early Church?" (*Liahona*, Feb. 2005); Patrick J. Kiger, "How Did the Apostles Die?" (*National Geographic*, Feb. 19, 2015).

## AN APPLICATION

*Do you actively live the gospel? Do you home or visit teach each month?*[90] *Are you a blessing to your ward and neighborhood?*

## THE SIXTH SEAL

"And I beheld when he had opened the sixth seal, and, lo, there was a great earthquake; and the sun became black as sackcloth of hair, and the moon became as blood; And the stars of heaven fell unto the earth, even as a fig tree casteth her untimely figs, when she is shaken of a mighty wind" (Rev. 6:12–13). This sixth seal appears to be our day, which will continue to be the focus of Revelation 7–19.

Elder Bruce R. McConkie overviewed many of the events that would take place during the first six seals of the earth's existence.[91] These included:

- Apostasy and Dark Ages
- Discovery and use of printing
- Protestant Reformation and age of Renaissance
- Discovery and colonization of America
- Establishment of the American nation
- Translation and printing of the Bible
- Establishment of the U.S. Constitution
- Latter-day revelation
- Coming forth of the Book of Mormon
- Opposition to the Book of Mormon
- Restoration of the priesthood and priesthood keys
- Restoration of the gospel
- Church and kingdom set up again
- Growth of the Church

---

90 In a legal contract, paragraph titles help to organize legal terms within the contract. At the end of the contract, there is one final clause stating that the paragraph titles are not binding as to the stipulations within each paragraph. In a gospel sense, *home teaching* is the paragraph title for the stipulations of *watching over, being with, and strengthening* the Church (see D&C 20:53) but home teaching itself should not be binding. Home teaching, therefore, is more than a monthly visit and a book report on the First Presidency article from the *Ensign*; some months, these two elements are necessary to *watch over, be with, and strengthen* assigned families, but in some months, other endeavors will be much more effective. Whatever the activity, as long as the home teacher is *watching over, being with, and strengthening* his assigned families, he has done his home teaching.

91 See Bruce R. McConkie, "Signs of the Times," *Mormon Doctrine* (Salt Lake City: Deseret Book, 1966), 1–14.

- Building of latter-day temples
- Lord to come suddenly to His temple
- Spirit of Elijah and genealogical research
- Persecution of the Saints
- Persecution of the Jews
- True gospel to be preached in all the world[92]
- Worldly knowledge to increase; scientific and inventive progress
- Disease, plague, and pestilence to sweep the earth
- Elements in commotion
- Disasters and calamities to abound
- Strikes, anarchy, and violence to increase
- Latter-day wickedness
- Spirit ceasing to strive with the wicked
- Famines, depressions, and economic turmoil
- Many false churches in latter days
- Lamanites to blossom as the rose

As you read this list of events that have happened and will happen, what feelings did you have? Excitement? Dread? Fear? Many people fear signs of the coming of the Lord; this fear might, in a roundabout way, imply that we aren't excited for Jesus to return. Certainly no Christian would ever say that he or she wasn't excited for Jesus to return, but when we dread the signs leading up to His return, we may be sending the wrong message about our feelings for that day.

Consider this comparison to winter. I personally hate cold winters. I don't snow ski or snowboard or ice skate (our first Christmas morning in Utah brought temperatures to twenty-six degrees below zero!). I admit

---

92 The scriptures teach that the gospel will be preached *in* all the world and not necessarily *to* all the people in the world *before* Jesus returns (see Matt. 24:14; Joseph Smith—Matthew 1:31). Technology allows the gospel to spread to every nation, kindred, tongue, and people (see Gary E. Stephenson, "The Knowledge of a Savior" [*BYU Women's Conference*, May 5, 2017].); there are increasing opportunities for people to hear the gospel in their own language (see D&C 90:11), but spreading the gospel will continue to go forward well after the Millennium has begun. In fact, one reason for the Savior's return is to provide an opportunity for all people on the earth to hear and receive the gospel and accept Jesus Christ as their Savior. This gathering of the Lord's people through preaching of the gospel will be historic. In fact, all previous gatherings will seem minuscule in comparison (see Jer. 16:14–17; 1 Ne. 22:24–25; 2 Ne. 9:2, 30:6–18; 3 Ne. 21:25–26).

that I've been a bit miserable each winter while living in Utah. However, let's say that my boss offered me a three-week long, all-expenses-paid vacation to Hawaii each winter once the temperatures stayed below freezing for ten consecutive days. How would my attitude and demeanor about winter change with this offer from my employer? Knowing me, I'd check the weather forecast each day once winter set in, *hoping* for cold so I could pack my bags for my trip. Rather than dreading wintertime, I would actually look forward to it. My feelings about winter and the cold wouldn't change, but because of the promise from my boss, my attitude and approach to winter would change dramatically.

Our feelings about the signs of the Second Coming and the events of the sixth seal might be the same way. If we could shift our attitude to one of excitement as we witness these events prophesied in Revelation 6 coming to pass, it might help us be better prepared for the Savior's arrival. And His coming will be *much* better than a three-week trip to Hawaii.

## AN APPLICATION

*Do you look forward to Jesus's Second Coming? If not, what can you do to become more excited about His arrival?*

## Revelation 7
### 144,000 AND MORE

BEFORE PROPHESYING THE JUDGMENTS THAT will come upon the unrepentant during the sixth seal, John saw an innumerable company of the righteous in Revelation 7, a powerful reminder that not all will suffer God's wrath. The question is asked in Revelation 6:17, "[W]ho shall be able to stand?" That is, who will be able to survive in the latter days during the sixth-seal events? Revelation 7:1 reads, "I saw four angels standing on the four corners of the earth, holding the four winds of the earth, that the wind should not blow on the earth, nor on the sea, nor on any tree," and Helaman chapter 5 gives an insight about the attributes of people who are able to stand during and despite calamities, or the winds that blow on the earth:

> And now, my sons, remember, remember that it is upon the rock of our Redeemer, who is Christ, the Son of God, that ye must build your foundation; that when the devil shall send forth his mighty winds, yea, his shafts in the whirlwind, yea, when all his hail and his mighty storm shall beat upon you, it shall have no power over you to drag you down to the gulf of misery and endless woe, because of the rock upon which ye are built, which is a sure foundation, a foundation whereon if men build they cannot fall. (Helaman 5:12)

When I was young, a painter came to repair a small crack in a wall of our home. It was patched and painted, but showed up again about a month later. My grandfather, a rather gruff retired Navy lieutenant, called him back and asked him to do it again. The same process was undertaken but again, about a month or two later, the crack was back in full view. My grandfather, now frustrated, called a different painter. The new painter arrived. He looked and looked and looked at the wall, not moving a muscle. Shaking his head, he told my grandfather that he wasn't the man for the job. My grandfather was a bit perplexed and asked why. The painter replied, "Sir, what you have isn't a patch and paint problem: it's a foundation problem. Your home's foundation is shifting. A patch will not help until you solidify your foundation." After a long process of securing our home's foundation, the crack was successfully repaired.

Let's look at the history behind our foundational (covenant) relationship with Christ. In the Old Testament, we read that Abraham received a covenant and blessing from the Lord (see Gen. 12:2–3 and Abr. 2:9–11) and passed it on to his son, Isaac. Isaac then bestowed this same blessing upon his son, Jacob, who was promised in Genesis 27:29: "[C]ursed be every one that curseth thee, and blessed be he that blesseth thee." In other words, the Lord promised to protect the posterity of Abraham, Isaac, and Jacob through their faithfulness to the covenant. We've seen the Lord protect and defend Abraham's seed and their promised land for the last 4000 years. The nation of Israel lies on a tiny strip of land surrounded by millions of people who have tried to sweep them off the earth (or into the Mediterranean Sea), and they haven't been successful for several millennia. Why? One reason is the Lord's promise to Abraham 4000 years ago.

As children of this same promise, we have been given the same blessing and condition. "And ye shall be my people, and I will be your God" (Jer. 30:22). As soon as we promise to make God *our* God and let Him rule and reign in our life, we become His people and heirs of the blessings promised to Abraham, Isaac, and Jacob.

In the parable of the wise man and the foolish man, who each build houses on different foundations (see Matt. 7:24–27), the house itself might represent a person's testimony, and the rock that the wise man's home was built on may represent the Savior. But what does the rain (which descended upon both of these houses) represent? Book of Mormon prophet Nephi gives this intriguing insight: "[W]o unto all those who tremble, and are angry because of the *truth of God*! For behold, he that is built upon the rock receiveth *it* with gladness; and he that is built upon a sandy foundation trembleth . . ." (2 Ne. 28:28, emphases added). According to Nephi, one symbol for the rain from the parable is the truth of God. The Lord, through the prophet Moses, taught, "My doctrine shall drop as the rain" (Deut. 32:2). Indeed, truth, like rain, falls upon everyone, but those whose lives are built and founded on Jesus Christ are able to receive truth (even truths or policies that are hard to understand) with confidence and gladness.

Alma taught about what happens to those who fully receive truth in Alma 26:

5. [T]hey shall be gathered into the garners, that they are not wasted.
6. Yea, they shall not be beaten down by the storm at the last day; yea, neither shall they be harrowed up by the whirlwinds; but when the storm cometh they shall be gathered together in their place, that the storm cannot penetrate to them; yea, neither shall they be driven with fierce winds whithersoever the enemy listeth to carry them.

What a beautiful set of promises from the Book of Mormon! President Wilford Woodruff similarly taught:

Can you tell me where the people are who will be shielded and protected from these great calamities and judgments which are even now at our doors? I'll tell you. [Those] who honor their priesthood, and who are worthy of their blessings are the only ones who shall have their safety and protection. They are the only mortal beings. No other people have a right to be shielded from these judgments. They are at our very doors; not even this people will escape them entirely. They will come down like the judgments of Sodom and Gomorrah. And none but the priesthood will be safe from their fury.[93]

The tribulation period recorded in Revelation 7 will last seven years over two three-and-a-half–year periods.[94] Although some of the righteous will endure second-hand suffering, it is clear that one characteristic of those who will be able to stand are those will have built their foundation on the

93 Wilford Woodruff, in *Young Women's Journal*, Aug. 1894, 512 as taken from Milton R. Hunter, *Pearl of Great Price Commentary: A Selection from the Revelations, Translations, and Narrations of Joseph Smith* (Salt Lake City: Bookcraft, 1948), 313–314.
94 See Dan. 7:25; Dan. 12:7,11; Rev. 11:2–3; Rev. 12:6,14; Rev. 13:5; Matt. 24:21–22.

rock of our Redeemer.[95] They will be those who honor the priesthood and faithfully sustain and follow priesthood leaders. This obedience will be key to enduring some of the calamities and tribulation of the days preceding the Second Coming. Our humble obedience to priesthood leaders and faithfulness to priesthood covenants will be critical if we are to stand firm.

A study of what *priesthood* means is instructive and inspiring. The suffix *hood* means *a current condition or state*. For example, *motherhood* is *a condition or state of being a mother*. So what does *priesthood* mean? It is simply *the quality or state of being a priest*. What, then, is a *priest*? The Latter-day Saint Bible Dictionary states that priests are "mediators between [us] and God." Therefore, *priesthood* could literally mean *the condition or state of being mediators between man and God*. When a priesthood holder home teaches or gives a priesthood blessing or administers the sacrament, he is literally acting as a mediator between those he serves and the God he serves. Following worthy and humble priesthood holders and priesthood leaders is one key to being guided through the latter-day storms, or tribulations, seen by John in Revelation 7.

## AN APPLICATION

*Do you sustain and honor priesthood leaders? Do you sustain the President of the Church and members of the Quorum of the Twelve Apostles as prophets, seers, and revelators? Do you sustain your stake president? Do you sustain your bishop or branch president?*

"And I saw another angel ascending from the east, having the seal of the living God," reads Revelation 7:2. Joseph Smith queried about this passage and received Doctrine and Covenants 77:11 in answer: "[T]hose who are sealed are high priests, ordained unto the holy order of God, to administer the everlasting gospel; for they are they who are ordained out of every nation, kindred, tongue, and people, by the angels to whom is given power over the nations of the earth, to bring as many as will come to the church of the Firstborn." The Prophet Joseph Smith went on to

---

95 Joseph Smith taught, "It is a false idea that the Saints will escape all the judgments, whilst the wicked suffer; for all flesh is subject to suffer, and 'the righteous shall hardly escape' . . . many of the righteous shall fall a prey to disease, to pestilence, etc., by reason of the weakness of the flesh, and yet be saved in the Kingdom of God." (*History of the Church,* 4:11); see also "Journals Series," *The Joseph Smith Papers,* vol. 1:1832–1839. Dean C. Jessee, Ronald K. Esplin, and Richard Lyman Bushman (eds). (Salt Lake City: The Church Historian's Press, 2008), 352–53.

teach that this event (ordination) "signifies sealing the blessings upon [the Saints'] heads, meaning the everlasting covenant, thereby making their calling and election sure."[96] Elder Bruce R. McConkie added, "Some of this sealing has already occurred—a few of Ephraim and a sprinkling of Manasseh have been sealed up unto eternal life; but the great day of fulfillment, where all Israel is concerned, lies ahead."[97]

Interestingly, Revelation 7:4–8 mentions 144,000 people who are saved (12,000 from each of the 12 tribes of Israel). Elder Orson Pratt taught, "These parties who are sealed in their foreheads will . . . gather up and hunt out the house of Israel, wherever they are scattered, and bring as many as they possibly can into the church of the [F]irstborn, preparatory to the great day of the coming of the Lord . . . Quite a host [of missionaries]."[98] However, Revelation 7:9 increases the number from 144,000 dramatically. "After this I beheld, and, lo, a great multitude, which no man could number, of all nations, and kindreds, and people, and tongues, stood before the throne." Certainly more than 144,000 will be involved in the latter-day hastening and much more than 144,000 people will be exalted!

What is interesting is the placement of the seal: *in* the forehead. It was a practice in John's day for devotees to mark their foreheads; followers of Zeus would mark their foreheads with the thunderbolt and followers of Poseidon with the trident. What's *inside* of our foreheads? Our minds. The frontal lobe is in the forefront of the brain and is located just behind the forehead. This part of the brain regulates decision-making, problem-solving, control of purposeful behaviors, consciousness, and emotions. The mind certainly is a key battleground to earning the celestial kingdom. If we can keep our mind centered on Christ and keep our thoughts clean and pure, I think we have a fighting chance to be able to withstand the latter-day calamities seen by John.

Our thoughts play a significant part in who we become. Proverbs 23:7 says, "For as [a man] thinketh in his heart, so is he." Those who are striving to be like the Savior make pure-mindedness a priority. Here are some helpful tips from the February 2001 *New Era* on how to keep our thoughts pure:

96 *Teachings of the Prophet Joseph Smith*, compiled by Joseph Fielding Smith (Salt Lake City: Deseret Book, 1977), 321.

97 Bruce R. McConkie, *The Millennial Messiah: The Second Coming of the Son of Man* (Salt Lake City: Deseret Book, 1982), 105.

98 Orson Pratt, "Gathering of Israel," *Journal of Discourses,* vol. 18, Delivered Apr. 11, 1875, 25.

- Reject a bad thought as soon as it comes into your mind, and it will be easier to do so the next time.
- Think good thoughts to crowd out the impure ones.
- Avoid watching, listening to, or reading any material that contains profanity, swearing, pornography, or other improper content.
- Make sure you choose your surroundings carefully and that your activities inspire good thoughts.
- Surround yourself with good friends who uphold Church standards.
- Pray. The Lord can help you overcome any problem you have, including unclean thoughts.
- Singing a hymn will elevate your thoughts. You could memorize a hymn you can turn to when you need to get rid of a bad thought.
- Remove yourself from situations where people are gossiping or using profane or vulgar language.[99]

There is a difference between thoughts in our mind and those that we choose to speak. The Savior taught, "Therefore take no thought, *saying*, What shall we eat? or, What shall we drink? or, Wherewithal shall we be clothed?" (Matt. 6:31, emphasis added). Once we talk about things, we give them life; when we articulate our problems we give them power. We should talk more about the promises than our problems. Rather than dwelling on the negative, we should focus on and speak about the positive. When we aren't promoted or when our hearts are broken or when other trials come our way, we should speak about how one door has been closed but God will open the next, all in an effort to keep our minds centered on Christ (2 Cor. 4:17–18).

On our television at home, I can tune in to over 200 stations. I do not just watch one channel over and over again, day after day. I love to surf around and find programs that interest me. If I do tune into a show and I'm not enjoying it, I am quick to change the channel and look for other programming. Our minds are very much the same. Often, we tune into one station and stay there. We are tempted to stay on a station of negativity or the channel of doubt, forgetting there are hundreds of other stations to turn to. When my mind becomes negative, I love to tune into stations like, *I have been blessed with a great family* or, *My wife sure loves me* or, *I can't wait until our next vacation.* Focusing on the negative programming

---

99 "Idea List: Clean Thoughts," *New Era*, Feb. 2011.

in our minds can breed negativity; tuning to other stations can bring joy. Strive always to keep the thoughts in your *forehead* positive and uplifting.

## AN APPLICATION

*Do you keep your thoughts clean, positive, and uplifting?*

Wrapping back into John's vision of the exalted in Revelation 7, John is asked by one of the elders (verse 13), "What are these which are arrayed in white robes? and whence came they?" And then the answer comes (verse 14): "These are they which came out of great tribulation, and have washed their robes, and made them white in the blood of the Lamb." In other words, those who actively access the purifying and sanctifying blessings of the Atonement of Jesus Christ are true victors.

Of this vast throng of valiant followers of the Savior who "came out of great tribulation, and have washed their robes, and made them white" (Rev. 7:14), President Spencer W. Kimball taught:

> It would seem that these people had not always been perfect. They had had soiled robes and many weaknesses, but had now overcome and had washed the soiled raiment in the blood of the Lamb. They were now clean and purified, as is indicated in the blessings promised.[100]

Christ cleanses, despite latter-day tribulation. In fact, through the power of Christ's Atonement, our earthly trials can not only be overcome but can even be turned to our benefit.

An example of this principle is the history of the codfish industry. At the turn of the century, codfish were in much demand, but there was a problem. How could people get the fish across the country and keep it fresh? They tried to freeze the fish and send it by rail, but it turned out to be very mushy and lacking flavor. Suppliers then tried to ship the fish live, turning railroad cars into huge saltwater aquariums. When the codfish arrived at their destinations, they were still alive but when they were prepared they were still mushy and tasteless. It was then remembered that the natural enemy to codfish was the catfish. The next experiment was to ship the codfish in the tanks along with a few catfish. Those catfish chased the codfish in the tank throughout the journey across the country to the

---

100 Spencer W. Kimball, *The Miracle of Forgiveness*, (Salt Lake City: Bookcraft, 1969), 354.

West Coast. This time, when the fish was prepared, they were flaky and had the same flavor as they did when they were caught fresh and prepared on the East Coast. You see, the catfish kept the cod from becoming stale. We, much like the codfish, need catfish (trials and tribulation) in our lives to keep us fresh and sharp.

**AN APPLICATION**

*Do you strive to stay faithful despite tribulation?*

# *Revelation 8*
## THE SIX JUDGMENTS

REVELATION 8:1 REVEALS THAT "THERE was silence in heaven about the space of half an hour." Doctrine and Covenants 88 also speaks of this silence in heaven:

> 95. And there shall be silence in heaven for the space of half an hour; and immediately after shall the curtain of heaven be unfolded, as a scroll is unfolded after it is rolled up, and the face of the Lord shall be unveiled;
> 96. And the saints that are upon the earth, who are alive, shall be quickened and be caught up to meet him.

As far as I have studied, we have no prophetic interpretation of Revelation 8:1 concerning what this silence in the space of half an hour is. However, an application comes to mind from the notably silent response from prophets in interpreting this verse: what do we do when the Lord is silent on a matter? Elder D. Todd Christofferson shared of one experience,

> I am grateful that there was not a quick solution to my problem. The fact that I was forced to turn to God for help almost daily over an extended period of years taught me truly how to pray and get answers to prayer and taught me a very practical way to have faith in God. I came to know my Savior and my Heavenly Father in a way . . . that might not have happened otherwise . . . I learned to trust the Lord with all my heart.[101]

---

101 D. Todd Christofferson, "Give Us This Day Our Daily Bread," *CES Fireside for Young Adults* Jan. 9, 2011, Brigham Young University.

When answers don't come, we should hold on and have faith in the things we do know to be true.

Elder Richard G. Hinckley of the Seventy shared a fantastic analogy:

> Some of you struggle with certain doctrines or practices of the Church, past or present; they just don't seem to quite fit for you. I say, so what? That's okay . . . *Be patient but be persistent.* Keep studying them, thinking about them, and praying about them. Everyone has questions. I suppose even the prophets themselves have had some questions. But don't throw away the jewels you do have in the meantime. Hold onto them; build on them. . . . Have you ever watched a stonemason build a rock wall? He will sometimes pick up a rock that just does not fit anywhere in the niches of the wall. But does he abandon the wall and walk away? No, he simply sets the rock aside and keeps building until a niche appears where it fits and then proceeds until the wall is finished. So perhaps should we temporarily set aside questions that we continue to struggle with and that we cannot quite seem to answer today, having faith that at some time in the future a niche will appear, in the rock wall of our testimony where they fit perfectly.[102]

## AN APPLICATION

*Are you patient when the Lord is silent?*

After the silence in Revelation 8:1, we read of the sounding of trumpets. Again, the Prophet Joseph Smith received clarity regarding this prophecy:

> 12. Q. What are we to understand by the sounding of the trumpets, mentioned in the 8th chapter of Revelation?
> A. We are to understand that as God made the world in six days, and on the seventh day he finished his work, and sanctified it, and also formed man out of the dust of the earth . . . the sounding of the trumpets of the seven angels are the preparing and finishing of his work, in the beginning of the seventh thousand years—the preparing of the way before the time of his coming. (D&C 77:12)

---

102 Richard G. Hinckley, "Prophetic Priorities," *BYU Devotional* May 15, 2007.

These trumpets in Revelation 8–9 and 19 signal the coming judgments on the earth:

First Angel's Trumpet
- Hail, fire, and blood are cast upon the earth (Rev. 8:7).

Second Angel's Trumpet
- A great burning mountain is cast into the sea and a third of sea creatures die (Rev. 8:8–9).

Third Angel's Trumpet
- A great star falls, affecting one-third of freshwater (Rev. 8:10–11).

Fourth Angel's Trumpet
- One-third of heavenly bodies are darkened (Rev. 8:12).

Fifth Angel's Trumpet
- The sun is darkened by smoke and a five-month battle ensues (Rev. 9:1–11).

Sixth Angel's Trumpet
- A thirteen-month war is fought (Rev. 9:13–21).

Seventh Angel's Trumpet
- Christ appears to the world (Rev. 19).

Doctrine and Covenants 88:88–89 reads,

88. And after your testimony cometh wrath and indignation upon the people.
89. For after your testimony cometh the testimony of earthquakes, that shall cause groanings in the midst of her, and men shall fall upon the ground and shall not be able to stand.

In essence, the Lord may be saying, "If you don't listen to the voice of my servants, the missionaries that I will send out before the Second Coming occurs, I will call them home, and then I'll preach my own sermon, and that sermon will be the voice of thunders and earthquakes and lightning and the sea heaving itself beyond its bound.

Which call do you like? The call of prophets or missionaries or bishops knocking at your door—or the Lord's voice of judgment and wrath? I had a young person at EFY raise her hand and reply to this question, "I'll take a *Monson* over a *monsoon* any day!"

How much divine shaking does it take to cause us to want to repent? Hopefully a still, small whispering of the Spirit will lead us to repent;

hopefully following the counsel of a priesthood leader is enough. Eventually, if we do not listen, the sounding of those trumpets is going to crescendo.

**AN APPLICATION**

*Do you seek repentance often? Do you quickly follow prophetic and local priesthood counsel when it's given?*

Next we learn in Revelation 8:13, "And I beheld, and heard an angel flying through the midst of heaven, saying with a loud voice, Woe, woe, woe, to the inhabiters of the earth by reason of the other voices of the trumpet of the three angels, which are yet to sound!" Notice the repetition of the word *woe*. If your childhood was similar to mine, when you were a little child and when your mom or dad caught you misbehaving and they called you by your first name, you knew you were in trouble. If you were called by your first *and* your last name, you were usually in *bigger* trouble. And if your mother or father called you by your first, middle, *and* last name, you were in *big* trouble! The Lord works very much the same way, using such emphasis to call our attention to His words. The three woes are also symbolic of the three appearances that Jesus will make during the time of His Second Coming:

First Appearance
- Christ will appear at Adam-ondi-Ahman (Dan. 7:9–10, 13–14; D&C 116).

Second Appearance
- The Savior will appear in Jerusalem during Armageddon (D&C 45:48, 51–53; Zech. 12:10, 14:2–5).

Third Appearance
- The Lord will appear in glory to all mankind (D&C 45:44; 101:23; Matt. 24:30; Isa. 40:5; Joseph Smith Translation Rev. 1:7).

# *Revelation 9*
## THE FIRST WOE: THE FIRST APPEARANCE

THE PROPHET JOSEPH SMITH ASKED in Doctrine and Covenants 77:13, "When are the things to be accomplished, which are written in the 9th chapter of Revelation?" And the Lord replied, "They are to be accomplished after the opening of the seventh seal, before the coming of Christ."

It can hardly be disputed that John saw modern-day warfare and means of transportation in Revelation 9:7–10. As we read this passage, let's try to visualize what John saw.

7. And the shapes of the locusts were like unto horses prepared unto battle; and on their heads were as it were crowns like gold, and their faces were as the faces of men.
8. And they had hair as the hair of women, and their teeth were as the teeth of lions.
9. And they had breastplates, as it were breastplates of iron; and the sound of their wings was as the sound of chariots of many horses running to battle.
10. And they had tails like unto scorpions, and there were stings in their tails: and their power was to hurt men five months.

John did a fantastic job describing what he saw of our modern-day warfare two thousand years ago, in terms familiar to the people of his day.

In Revelation 9:21, John describes the reasons behind the destruction: "Neither repented they of their murders, nor of their sorceries, nor of their fornication, nor of their thefts." Simply stated, the Lord's destruction was sent as a consequence of sinning.

Concerning the nature of sin, 1 John 1:7 teaches that "the blood of Jesus Christ his Son cleanses us from all *sin*" (emphasis added). *Sin*, singular, refers to the powerful nature of sin within us. We can think of this as a tree of *sin* that produces fruit of *sins*. *Sins*, plural, refers to acts of sinning, or the fruits of our sinful nature being manifest. As promised by John in 1 John 1:7, "the blood of Jesus Christ his Son cleanses us from all sin." Verse 9 adds a clause: "If we confess our *sins*, he is faithful and just to forgive us our sins and cleanse us from all unrighteousness." *Sin* is the disease and *sins* are the symptoms—and the Atonement can take care of both.

This passage in Revelation 9:21 lists the four most prominent sins of the latter days: murders, sorceries, fornication, and thefts. The first of these sins, murder, is prominent in our day. From senseless acts of violence to terrorism and school shootings, there are many methods of murder occurring in and being justified by our society today.

The second prominent sin listed by John is *sorceries*. Certainly there are undertones of devil-worshipping and occult activity when we read that word; interestingly, however, the way *sorceries* is used here in Revelation 9:21 may also refer to drug use. The Greek word for *sorcery* used here is *pharmakeia*, which had reference to witchcraft, poisoning, and administering drugs.[103] The words *pharmacy* and *pharmaceutical* are derived from *pharmakeia*. As the use and abuse of methamphetamine and opioids grow, we may be seeing fulfillment of John's prophetic vision.

The third prominent sin listed is immorality. *Porneia* is the Greek word used in this verse (the root of the English terms *pornography*) and refers to sexual activity outside of marriage. In our day, rampant use of pornographic materials fosters immorality and threatens marriage.

The fourth major sin of the latter days will be thievery. Crime in all of its manifestations is on the upsurge today, from theft of personal property to digital theft of data to identify theft.

**AN APPLICATION**

*Are you free from media glorifying murder for entertainment purposes? Are you clean of drug abuse? Are you free from pornography? Are you free from stealing?*

As these sins and crimes and wars rage in the last days, the Savior will appear to a select group at Adam-ondi-Ahman. This is uniquely Latter-day Saint doctrine. Speaking of the events at Adam-ondi-Ahman, Elder Bruce R. McConkie taught, "[B]efore any of his appearances . . . there is to be a secret appearance to selected members of his Church. He will come in private to his prophet and to the apostles then living. Those who have held

---

103 "Pharmakeia," *BLB Classic*, accessed June 19, 2017, www.blueletterbible.org.

keys and powers and authorities in all ages from Adam to the present will also be present."[104] He later explained:

> *Ahman* is one of the names by which God was known to Adam. *Adam-ondi-Ahman*, a name carried over from the pure Adamic language into English, is one for which we have not been given a revealed, literal translation. As near as we can judge—and this view comes down from the early brethren who associated with the Prophet Joseph Smith, who was the first one to use the name in this dispensation—*Adam-ondi-Ahman* means *the place or land of God where Adam dwelt.*[105]

Doctrinally, it has been revealed that both men and women will be present at the assembly at Adam-ondi-Ahman.[106] While there, the Saints will be prepared to live in a paradisiacal glory and "Adam-ondi-Ahman will be the most momentous event of this earth" and will "adjust the affairs of the entire world."[107,108,109] Elder Orson Pratt taught that without Adam-ondi-Ahman, everything would be in confusion at the Second Coming of the Lord.[110]

The sacrament will be administered at Adam-ondi-Ahman, according to Doctrine and Covenants 27:5, which reads, "[F]or the hour cometh that I will drink of the fruit of the vine with you on the earth." Imagine being at this sacrament service! Let's say you were asked to prepare the sacrament meeting agenda for this gathering. Who would you invite to speak at that meeting? Would you have Adam speak on the Fall? Would you invite Moses to talk about commandments? Might you ask John to talk about the

---

104 Bruce R. McConkie, *The Millennial Messiah: The Second Coming of the Son of Man* (Salt Lake City: Deseret Book, 1982), 578–79.
105 Bruce R. McConkie, *Mormon Doctrine* (Salt Lake City: Deseret Book, 1966), 19–20.
106 Bruce R. McConkie, *The Millennial Messiah: The Second Coming of the Son of Man* (Salt Lake City: Deseret Book, 1982), 581.
107 Bruce R. McConkie, *The Millennial Messiah: The Second Coming of the Son of Man* (Salt Lake City: Deseret Book, 1982), 585–86.
108 Joseph Fielding Smith, *The Way to Perfection* (Salt Lake City: Deseret Book, 1984), 289.
109 John Taylor, *The Gospel Kingdom* (Salt Lake City: Bookcraft, 1987), 216–17.
110 Orson Pratt, *Journal of Discourses,* vol. 18 (Delivered Feb. 25, 1877), 344.

Aaronic Priesthood? Would you consider having Joseph Smith speak on the Restoration of the gospel? Might you invite Enoch to speak on Zion? Doctrine and Covenants 27:5–12 provides a partial list of invitees to this event. Some notables include Moroni, Elias, John, Elijah, Abraham, Isaac, Jacob, Joseph, and Michael.

Doctrine and Covenants 27:15–18 provides the dress code for this event: the armor of God. President Harold B. Lee taught:

> We have the four parts of the body that the Apostle Paul said [are] the most vulnerable to the powers of darkness. The loins, typifying virtue, chastity. The heart, typifying our conduct. Our feet, our goals or objectives in life. And finally our head, our thoughts.[111]

What a beautiful time this is going to be at Adam-ondi-Ahman! And what preparations the Lord is making for this meeting.

To look for principles relevant to us from the gathering at Adam-ondi-Ahman, sacrament meeting practices come to mind. Prophets have given several suggestions for improving our sacrament meeting experiences. Elder Dallin H. Oaks taught,

> This is not a time for conversation or transmission of messages but a period of prayerful meditation as . . . members prepare spiritually for the sacrament. . . . During sacrament meeting—and especially during the sacrament service—we should concentrate on worship and refrain from all other activities, especially from behavior that could interfere with the worship of others . . . Sacrament meeting is not a time for reading books or magazines . . . it is not a time for whispered conversations on cell phones or for texting.[112]

## AN APPLICATION

*Do you attend your sacrament meeting and other meetings? How well do you prepare for this worship service?*

---

111 Harold B. Lee, "Feet Shod with the Preparation of the Gospel of Peace," Brigham Young University Speeches of the Year (Nov. 9, 1954), 2.
112 Dallin H. Oaks, "Sacrament Meeting and the Sacrament," *Ensign*, Nov. 2008.

As Latter-day Saints, we believe wholeheartedly in the doctrine and power of gathering. The Apostle Paul in the book of Hebrews commands us to not "[forsake] the assembling of ourselves together" (Heb. 10:25). In the following verses from Doctrine and Covenants 44, we are given the reasons behind the command to gather:

1. [I]t is expedient in me that the elders of my church should be called together.
2. And it shall come to pass, that inasmuch they are faithful, and exercise faith in me, I will pour out my Spirit upon them in the day that they assemble themselves together.
5. That your enemies may not have power over you; that you may be preserved in all things; that you may be enabled to keep my laws; that every bond may be broken wherewith the enemy seeketh to destroy my people.

Elder David A. Bednar taught that there are four purposes of gathering: (1) To worship (Mosiah 18:25), (2) to build up the Church (D&C 101:63–64), (3) for a defense (D&C 115:6), and (4) to receive counsel and instruction (Mosiah 18:7).[113] Like penguins that huddle in the subzero temperature to stay warm, geese that reduce their drag by flying in formation, or tall redwood trees that intertwine their roots to resist wind and storms; when we unite to worship as congregations, we are blessed, strengthened, and protected further than when we do not gather together.

One event that will occur before the Savior's return is the building of a temple in Jerusalem and in the New Jerusalem. The first temple in Jerusalem was Solomon's temple (destroyed by the Babylonians in 586 B.C.). The second temple in Jerusalem, known as "Herod's Temple," was commissioned by Cyrus (destroyed by the Romans in A.D. 70). The third and fourth temples will be at Jerusalem and the other at the New Jerusalem in Independence, Missouri.[114]

The restoration of the tribe of Judah and the city of Jerusalem appears as an important theme in Old Testament and Book of Mormon

---

113 David A. Bednar, "The Spirit and Purposes of Gathering," *Brigham Young University—Idaho Devotional*, Oct. 31, 2006.

114 The Temple Lot site, dedicated by the Prophet Joseph Smith for the Independence Temple, is in Independence, Missouri. Church of Christ headquarters is on site (see "Independence Temple," *Temples of The Church of Jesus Christ of Latter-day Saints*, accessed Jun. 8, 2017, ldschurchtemples.org/independence).

prophecy.[115] Of that, Joseph Smith taught, "Judah must return, Jerusalem must be rebuilt, and the temple, and water come out from under the temple, and the waters of the Dead Sea be healed. It will take some time to rebuild the walls of the city and the temple, &c.; and all this must be done before the Son of Man will make His appearance."[116]

Revelation 9:12 sets the stage for the second and third visitations of the Savior following Adam-ondi-Ahman: "One woe is past; and, behold, there come two woes more hereafter."

115 Elder Bruce R. McConkie explained that the current gathering of the Jews to their homeland is not a fulfillment of this prophecy, but a political gathering. "As all the world knows, many Jews are now gathering to Palestine, where they have their own nation and way of worship, all without reference to a belief in Christ or an acceptance of the laws and ordinances of His everlasting gospel. Is this the latter-day gathering of the Jews of which the scriptures speak? No! It is not; let there be no misunderstanding in any discerning mind on this point. This gathering of the Jews to their homeland, and their organization into a nation and a kingdom, is not the gathering promised by the prophets. It does not fulfill the ancient promises. Those who have thus assembled have not gathered into the true Church and fold of their ancient Messiah" (Bruce R. McConkie, *The Millennial Messiah: The Second Coming of the Son of Man* [Salt Lake City: Deseret Book, 1982], 229.).
116 *History of the Church*, vol. 5, 337.

*Revelation 10*
## THE LITTLE BOOK

IN REVELATION 10, AN ANGEL gave John a little book to symbolically eat. This *little book* interlude seems to be a pause in John's vision. "What are we to understand by the little book which was eaten by John, as mentioned in the 10th chapter of Revelation?" inquired the Prophet Joseph Smith in Doctrine and Covenants 77:14. The Lord answered that "We are to understand that it was a mission, and an ordinance, for him to gather the tribes of Israel; behold, this is Elias, who, as it is written, must come and restore all things." Since John was to live through all the events he saw as a translated being, the Lord seems to pause to show him what role he will play in these prophecies.[117]

As we know, John's mission was to gather the twelve tribes of Israel during his ministry, and then his mission continued with his appearance to Joseph Smith and Oliver Cowdery to assist in restoring the Melchizedek Priesthood. Surely his work will continue into the Millennium (see John 21:20–23; D&C 27:12).

In fact, here in Revelation 10, John is given a sneak peek at the events that will occur during the Millennium, starting with the resurrection of the dead. In Revelation 10:1, John saw a strong angel coming down out of heaven. This mighty angel is clothed with a cloud, symbolic of God's glory (see Ex. 16:10; Lev. 16:2; 1 Kgs. 8:10; Ezek. 10:4) or God's judgment (see Matt. 24:30, 26:64; Mark 13:26, 14:62; Luke 21:27; Rev. 1:7, 14:14–16). This angel has a rainbow upon his head, which may signifying His faithfulness and mercy (see Gen. 9:12–17). The angel's face is like the sun and his feet like pillars of fire. *Pillars of fire* are reminiscent of Israel's wilderness wanderings, when God sent a pillar of fire to guide

---

117 In a similar fashion, after Church members are sustained and set apart for callings, they too are given books (i.e., a handbook) to assist them in their new assignments.

the Israelites at night and a cloud by day (Ex. 13:21–22). Hence, this angel—signifying judgment, glory, and power—is sent to not only guide, but also to deliver and protect God's people (Ex. 14:24). The angel, according to Revelation 10:2, has a little book in his hand that he gives to John to read.

As John reads, he learns of seven trumpets beginning to sound (Rev. 10:4). Latter-day revelation records that these trumpets signal the beginning of the resurrections.[118] At the sounding of the first angel's trumpet, all who are celestial spirits will be resurrected (D&C 88:28). At the next trumpet's sound, the resurrection of terrestrial beings will occur (D&C 88:99). The third trumpet (D&C 88:100–101) will bring forth those who will be in the telestial kingdom.[119] Then the resurrection of the sons of perdition will occur (D&C 88:102).

After witnessing these resurrection events, the angel calls out with a loud voice and the sound is like a lion roaring or like thunder. John is about to write down what the seven thunders said, but a voice commands John to simply seal the message up (see Rev. 10:3–4). John is instead commanded in Revelation 10:8–9 to "Go and take the little book . . . and eat it up; and it shall make thy belly bitter, but it shall be in thy mouth sweet as honey."[120] The book that John ate was both bitter and sweet—bitter because many would reject the gospel of Christ and suffer the judgments of God, and sweet because so many souls will be saved by his ministry among the house of Israel.[121] Perhaps it seems strange to eat a book, but Ezekiel was also asked to eat a book. His assignment was similar

---

118 While John was commanded not to write down these events, the Prophet Joseph received a similar vision of these events and was permitted to provide detail (see D&C 88).

119 Joseph Fielding Smith, compiled by Bruce R. McConkie, *Doctrines of Salvation*, vol. 2 (Salt Lake City: Bookcraft, 1992), 302.

120 D&C 88 reveals that the angel communicating with John is Michael, as the same events found in Rev. 10 are paralleled in section 88.

121 Joseph Smith wrote about truth tasting *sweet,* as follows: "This is good doctrine. It tastes good. I can taste the principles of eternal life, and so can you. They are given to me by the revelations of Jesus Christ; and I know that when I tell you these words of eternal life as they are given to me, you taste them, and I know that you believe them. You say honey is sweet, and so do I. I can also taste the spirit of eternal life. I know it is good; and when I tell you of these things which were given me by inspiration of the Holy Spirit, you are bound to receive them as sweet, and rejoice more and more." (*Teachings of the Prophet Joseph Smith*, compiled by Joseph Fielding Smith [Salt Lake City: Deseret Book, 1977], 355).

to John's: "And when I looked, behold . . . and, lo, a roll of a book was therein; And he spread it before me; and . . . said . . . eat this roll, and go speak unto the house of Israel. So I opened my mouth, and he caused me to eat that roll" (Ezek. 2:9–10, 3:1–2).

The imagery of eating scriptures can point our minds to the scriptural command to "feast upon the words of Christ" (2 Ne. 32:3). This implies much more than just casually reading the scriptures. We should search them, pondering what they teach, and then liken the principles and doctrines to ourselves. Eating is a universal idiom for receiving knowledge, but scriptural knowledge is not merely knowing for the sake of knowing; it implies application into one's life. You may have heard the old adage, "You are what you eat." Well, it's true: when a person eats an apple, the body metabolizes it. It assimilates and converts it to energy. We literally bear our food on our body. The same ought to be true with scripture: as we digest the word of God, we should begin to act like and have a countenance more fully resembling that of Jesus Christ. Meaningful study of the scriptures can build our faith, fortify us against temptation, and help us be prepared to share the gospel with others if we apply what we read.

Scriptures are powerful. One of the first things Joseph Smith noted after leaving the Sacred Grove was not his feelings about God or about having seen the Savior or the power of prayer. He said, "I had found the testimony of James to be true—that a man who lacked wisdom might ask of God, obtain wisdom, and not be upbraided" (JS—H 1:26).[122] What a great testimony of the power of scriptures! Among the first things the Prophet Joseph testified of was the power of scripture study.

Sister Celia Cruz Ayala shared her witness of the power of scriptures. A man attacked her, stealing her purse and a wrapped copy of the Book of Mormon. She received the following letter only days later:

> Mrs. Cruz:
> Forgive me, forgive me. You will never know how sorry I am for attacking you . . . I want you to know that you seemed to have a radiance about you. That light seemed to stop me [from harming you, so] I ran away instead.
> I want you to know that you will see me again, but when you do, you won't recognize me, for I will be your

---

122 For a more complete account of Joseph Smith's story, see Joseph Smith—History in the Pearl of Great Price, or *History of the Church* 1:2–79.

brother. . . . Here, where I live, I have to find the Lord and go to the church you belong to.

The message you wrote in [the Book of Mormon] brought tears to my eyes . . . I have not been able to stop reading it. I have prayed and asked God to forgive me, [and] I ask you to forgive me. . . .
—Your absent friend.[123]

In the old time Western movies, scenes of conflict between cowboys and Native Americans filled the screens. The cowboys would wield their guns and the Indians would shoot their arrows. Quite often, the cowboys would circle their wagons and set up a defense against the Indians. They used the canvas coverings of their wagons to protect themselves from the arrows of the Indians. Many of those early movies showed one of the Native American leaders wrapping his arrow in cloth and then dipping the tip into tar or sap. The Native American would then light the tip of the arrow on fire. His intent from lighting his arrow and then firing it toward the cowboys was to ignite the protective wagon covering, exposing the cowboys to the piercing arrows.

The fiery darts spoken of in the scriptures are similarly aimed to weaken defenses—in this case, they are intended to destroy us spiritually. Fortunately, when the devil sends his fiery darts our way, the Lord has equipped us with stronger weaponry. In addition to our shield of faith and the other pieces of armor (Eph. 6:10–18), we also have the sword of the spirit, which is the word of God. Our only offensive weapon is the scriptures. In 1 Nephi 15:24, we are taught that "whoso [hearkens] unto the word of God and [holds] fast unto it, they [will] never perish; neither [can] the temptations and the fiery darts of the adversary overpower them unto blindness, to lead them away to destruction."

A key to success when it comes to battling Satan is our commitment to study and apply the word of God consistently—daily. Scripture study and application keeps us safe and secure when those fiery darts of temptation and distraction shoot into our lives. "For the word of God is quick, and powerful, and sharper than any twoedged sword, piercing even to the dividing asunder of soul and spirit, and of the joints and marrow, and is a discerner of the thoughts and intents of the heart" (Heb. 4:12).

To make our study more meaningful as we *eat* our *little books*, we may choose to look for deeper meaning in a verse of scripture by asking questions

123 F. Burton Howard, "My Life Has Changed," *Church News* Jan. 6, 1996, 16.

that help us to think more deeply about what it teaches. We may choose to use the footnotes, the Topical Guide, the Bible Dictionary, and the Guide to the Scriptures to gain insights into the verses read. The seminary and institute manuals are also excellent resources. As you read, consider how scriptural accounts and teachings apply to your life, search for meaningful words and phrases, seek answers to questions you have, and ponder insights about gospel principles. When a word or phrase in the scriptures impresses you, mark it. Keep a journal of the insights, feelings, and impressions you receive as you study the scriptures or eat your little book.

Scriptures are potent. Never let a day go by without studying scripture. Why? Because a day will not go by that Satan will not shoot a fiery dart in our direction!

**AN APPLICATION**

*How would you rate your personal scripture study?*

## *Revelation 11*
## THE SECOND WOE: THE TWO WITNESSES

PARLEY P. PRATT PROVIDED AN overview of Revelation 11 when he penned:

> [T]he Jews gather home, and rebuild Jerusalem. The nations gather against them in battle . . . Prophets . . . are slain, and the city is left in a great measure to the mercy of their enemies for three days and a half, the two Prophets rise from the dead and ascend into heaven. The Messiah comes, convulses the earth, overthrows the army of the Gentiles, delivers the Jews, [and] cleanses Jerusalem.[124]

There are two prophets spoken of in Revelation 11. Joseph Smith asked in Doctrine and Covenants 77, "What is to be understood by the two witnesses, in the eleventh chapter of Revelation?" The answer from verse 15 reads, "They are two prophets that are to be raised up to the Jewish nation in the last days, at the time of the restoration, and to prophesy to the Jews after they are gathered and have built the city of Jerusalem in the land of their fathers." Regarding these two prophets, Revelation 11:3 and 5 reveal, "I will give power to my two witnesses, and they shall prophesy a thousand two hundred and threescore days, clothed in sackcloth.[125] . . . And if any

---

124 David B. Galbraith, D. Kelly Ogden, Andrew C. Skinner, *Jerusalem: The Eternal City* (Salt Lake City: Deseret Book, 1996), 536.

125 This three-and-one-half-year period mentioned in Revelation 11:2 will be one of apostasy when the Lord's work will be symbolically trampled on. Revelation 11:3 indicates that two witnesses will serve an assignment in Jerusalem, balancing the time of apostasy with the time of their preaching, giving people an equal opportunity to choose the Lord or those in opposition to Him (see "Rev. 11: Two Special Witnesses," *New Testament Student Study Guide* (Salt Lake City: The Church of Jesus Christ of Latter-day Saints, 2003), 170.

man will hurt them, fire proceedeth out of their mouth, and devoureth their enemies" (see verses 3–12).[126]

There are similarities between the ministry of these two witnesses and that of Christ's ministry: they will preach to the Jews, they will be persecuted, they will be killed by the Jews, and they will be resurrected and ascend into heaven.

Who are the two witnesses? Elder Bruce R. McConkie, in his *Doctrinal New Testament Commentary*, wrote:

> These two shall be followers of that humble man Joseph Smith, through whom the Lord of Heaven restored the fullness of his everlasting gospel in this final dispensation of grace. No doubt they will be members of the Council of the Twelve or of the First Presidency of the Church.[127]

When they have finished their testimony, these two witnesses will be killed. Meanwhile, "[T]hey that dwell upon the earth shall rejoice over them, and make merry, and shall send gifts one to another; because these two prophets tormented them that dwelt on the earth" (Rev. 11:10). There will be a point during the ministry of these two prophets when evil seems to have won, but that will be shattered in an instant: "After three days and a half the Spirit of life from God entered into them, and they stood upon their feet, *and great fear fell upon them which saw them.* And they heard a great voice from heaven saying unto them, Come up hither. And they ascended up to heaven in a cloud; and their enemies beheld them" (Rev. 11:11–12, emphasis added; see also verse 13).

Recall the prophecy of the Prophet Joseph Smith regarding the Church of God in the latter days:

> [N]o unhallowed hand can stop the work from pro-
> gressing; persecutions may rage, mobs may combine,
> armies may assemble, calumny may defame, but the truth
> of God will go forth boldly, nobly, and independent, till it
> has penetrated every continent, visited every clime, swept

---

126 This is most likely symbolic. Prophets breathing fire sounds improbable, although all things are possible with the Lord; it is possible that these two prophets' method of teaching will cause "the Spirit of God like a fire [to burn]" (See "The Spirit of God," *Hymns*, no. 2.

127 Bruce R. McConkie, *Doctrinal New Testament Commentary*, vol. 3 (Salt Lake City: Deseret Book, 2002), 509.

every country, and sounded in every ear, till the purposes of God shall be accomplished, and the Great Jehovah shall say the work is done.[128]

One message in Revelation 11 is that hope is *never* lost. Many people today continue to hope for blessings, miracles, and divine intervention. Elder Jeffrey R. Holland encourages: "[I]f the bitter cup does not pass, drink it and be strong, trusting in happier days ahead."[129] From newly called missionaries to young mothers and fathers to single parents who feel like it is them against the world, the faithful find a way. From young single adults who aren't married but wish to be, to people who desire to have children and cannot, Elder Holland invites:

> Cling to your faith. Hold on to your hope . . . [Remember the greats like] Abraham, [who] "against [all] hope believed in hope" and "staggered not . . . through unbelief." . . .
>
> Even if you cannot always see that silver lining on your clouds, God can . . . He is your Heavenly Father, and surely He matches with His own the tears His children shed.[130]

Doctrine and Covenants 88:68 declares that some experiences will come to us "in his own time, and in his own way, and according to his own will." Have complete faith in God's divine timetable. Trust the Lord and be absolutely patient with His timing. He *is* coming! This message of hope despite trials and momentary setbacks resonates from the verses of Revelation 11.

### AN APPLICATION

*Do you have faith in God's timetable? Do you cling to hope when all seems lost or doomed?*

The following prophecies will be fulfilled around the time of the second woe, which is the second appearance of the Savior:

- The land of Israel will be reinhabited by the covenant people (Ezek. 36:10–12, 33–36).

---

128 Joseph Smith, *History of the Church,* vol. 4, 540.
129 Elder Jeffrey R. Holland, "Like a Broken Vessel," *Ensign,* Nov. 2013.
130 Ibid.

- The land will become highly productive and fruitful (Ezek. 36:8, 29–30, 34–35).
- There will be one nation in the land of Israel again (Ezek. 37:22).
- Jerusalem will be reestablished as the capital city of the Israelites (Zech. 1:16–17; 2:12; 12:6).
- Judah will become powerful in politics and warfare (Isa. 19:16–17; Zech. 10:3, 5–6).

Revelation 11:14 reads, "The second woe is past; and, behold, the third woe cometh quickly."

CHAPTERS 12 THROUGH 14 OF the book of Revelation are another break in John's panoramic vision. As evident in these three chapters, John saw a woman (who represents the Church and the ecclesiastical portion of the Lord's dominion) bring forth a kingdom over which Christ reigns as king (Rev. 12:1–3, 7). John then saw that the Church and kingdom of God (or Zion) were opposed by the great dragon (Satan) and taken away for many years (Rev. 12:4–5). This means that the Church of John's day would not bring forth the kingdom but would be driven into the wilderness (apostasy) by the dragon.[131]

Note that the dragon has ten horns (symbols of temporary domination and partial power). This is not true of the Lamb, whom John depicts as having seven horns (the symbols of fullness; see *Appendix: Symbolism of Numbers*). John's metaphor shows that the dragon is indeed powerful, but the Lamb is more so and will eventually overcome and destroy the dragon, as we will see towards the end of the book of Revelation.

After writing of his vision of the great battle of Armageddon in the preceding chapter, John wrote in Revelation 12 of when the battle actually began: that is, the premortal existence. He was shown through vision the role of the Lamb and the role of the dragon:

> 7. And there was war in heaven: Michael and his angels fought against the dragon; and the dragon fought and his angels,
> 8. And prevailed not; neither was their place found any more in heaven.

---

131 The Greek word *drakōn* signifies a serpent or sea monster that opposes God and all that is holy. This symbol is in stark contrast to the woman who brought forth the kingdom of God. See also Rev. 12:13–17; D&C 5:14, 33:5, 86:1–3; Jacob 5.

9. And the great dragon was cast out, that old serpent, called the Devil, and Satan, which deceiveth the whole world: he was cast out into the earth, and his angels were cast out with him.
10. And I heard a loud voice saying in heaven, Now is come salvation, and strength, and the kingdom of our God, and the power of his Christ: for the accuser of our brethren is cast down, which accused them before our God day and night.
11. And they overcame him by the blood of the Lamb, and by the word of their testimony; and they loved not their lives unto the death.

Simply stated, the war in Revelation 12 is for the souls of men. Revelation 12:7–11 helps us understand the nature of our enemy by listing a few of his evil titles. The first is *dragon* (verse 7). The Greek word used here is *drákōn*, which means *to see* or *seeing one*.[132] Another title given to him is Satan (verse 9). The Greek term for *Satan* means *the adversary* or *opposition*.[133] Then comes the name *Lucifer*, which means *Lightbringer* (see "Devil," *Bible Dictionary*).

The Greek Septuagint translates *devil* as *diabolos,* which means *slanderer*. This term literally means, "one who throws something across the path of another."[134] This definition is dripping with personal application.

When a moment of disaccord occurs, there is a moment of decision. If a person chooses to take offense by the *slander* of another, he or she will be tempted to build a wall and harden his or her heart against forgiveness. This is a sinful practice. We must, when accusation and contention arise, choose to act and avoid reacting. When someone wrongs us or doesn't handle something the way we wish they would have, we need to avoid erecting walls and hardening our hearts—doing so allows Satan to place a wedge in the relationship through his slander. Elder Neal A. Maxwell taught that "we should not make an individual 'an offender for a word' (Isa. 29:21; 2 Ne. 27:32), as if a single communication could set aside all else an individual may have communicated or stood for!"[135]

Notice another title for Lucifer: "the accuser of our brethren" (Rev. 12:10). What did Lucifer accuse us and our brothers and sisters of in the

---

132 "Dragon." In *Strong's Concordance*, accessed June 19, 2017, biblehub.com/greek/1404.htm.
133 "Satan." In *Strong's Concordance*, accessed June 19, 2017, biblehub.com/greek/4566.htm.
134" Satan." In *Online Etymology Dictionary*, accessed June 19, 2017, www.etymonline.com.
135 Neal A. Maxwell, "Out of Obscurity," *Ensign*, Nov. 1984, 8.

pre-earth life? It's easy and natural to picture Lucifer pointing, jeering, and taunting, "Do you think you're good enough to go down and repent of every sin that you commit? You think you can live a good life and make it back to Father's presence? You're going to have not only agency, but also a body that you're not going to be able to control very well. You think you can make it back safe and sound?" Further, it's easy to imagine Lucifer—the adversary, with his satanic and accusatory finger waving around mercilessly in the pre-earth courts—accusing the Messiah, "Do you think you can live a perfect, sinless life, not even one single mistake, not an unworthy thought? Do you really think you can do that and make an atonement for people who may not even accept your offering?" Latter-day Saint author Stephen Robinson further explained:

> Satan is the archetypical prosecutor or attorney for the plaintiff. He's an accuser, a prosecutor—he never defends. Satan is an inquisitor; he finds fault, and where he finds no actual fault, he cleverly creates the appearance of fault. That is what Satan is; it's what he does; it is his essence to lie and to accuse, and his lying accusations *will often seem correct* to most honest, objective observers . . . We should not be surprised to see the Brethren in our day, the Lord's anointed in the modern Church, attacked with false accusations in the media of the world. That is what Satan does, what he has done from the beginning.[136]

Al Fox Caraway, better known as the Tattooed Mormon, converted to the gospel in New York City and then moved to Utah. Shortly after she arrived, she had a disheartening experience while buying a book at a Church-owned bookstore. She recounts, "I was holding a church book in my hands. It was a biography on one of the prophets. And while I was waiting in line I felt very tense. I could *feel* stares [from] every direction; it felt like lasers. I stood there stiff trying to ignore it but I couldn't. I could physically feel the stares from everyone. Finally, the guy next to me tapped me on the arm and said, 'You know . . . it's pretty ironic you look the way you do holding *that* book.'"[137] Elder Jeffrey R. Holland admonishes us:

---

136 *Following Christ: The Parable of the Divers and More Good News* (Salt Lake City: Deseret Book, 1995), 115.
137 Al Fox Carraway, "Tattooed Mormon," *In the Head of Al*, accessed Jun. 8, 2017, alfoxshead.blogspot.com/2013/04/tattooed-mormon.html.

*Let people repent. Let people grow. Believe that people can change and improve* . . . If something is buried in the past, leave it buried. Don't keep going back with your little sand pail and beach shovel to dig it up, wave it around, and then throw it at someone, saying, "Hey! Do you remember *this?*" Splat!

Well, guess what? That is probably going to result in some ugly morsel being dug up out of *your* landfill with the reply, "Yeah, I remember it. Do *you* remember *this?*" Splat.

And soon enough everyone comes out of that exchange dirty and muddy and unhappy and hurt, when what our Father in Heaven pleads for is cleanliness and kindness and happiness and healing.[138]

Elder Marvin J. Ashton explained:

Perhaps the greatest charity comes when we are kind to each other, when we don't judge or categorize someone else, when we simply give each other the benefit of the doubt or remain quiet. Charity is accepting someone's differences, weaknesses, and shortcomings; having patience with someone who has let us down; or resisting the impulse to become offended when someone doesn't handle something the way we might have hoped. Charity is refusing to take advantage of another's weakness and being willing to forgive someone who has hurt us. Charity is expecting the best of each other.[139]

In 1 Corinthians 13:5, we learn that love "is not easily provoked." The Greek phrase is literally, *Love does not impute evil.* The word *impute* is translated as *logidzomai*, which is the same word that is used to define how God credits the righteousness of Christ to our account (imputation). *Logidzomai* is an accounting term, so the beautiful phrase from Corinthians that teaches that love is not easily provoked could translate as, *Love does not keep a ledger of wrongs done to us.* Love does not keep score. Love doesn't

138 Jeffrey R. Holland, "The Best is Yet to Be," *Ensign,* Jan. 2010.
139 Marvin J. Ashton, "The Tongue Can Be a Sharp Sword," *Ensign,* May 1992.

care who is right, who is first, who should apologize first, who should extend the hand of forgiveness first.

To be clear, forgiving others is not about ignoring or rationalizing wrongs. Forgiveness doesn't require us to downplay the offense, and neither is it surrendering our desire for justice; vengeance, however, or a desire to hurt those who have hurt us, is very different from justice. Forgiving is also not forgetting. Forgetting is physiological, while forgiveness is spiritual. Finally, forgiveness is not reconciliation. Forgiveness has no strings attached, but reconciliation does because it requires the involvement of both parties (the offender and the victim). Forgiveness, unlike reconciliation, can be offered to anyone, even if they don't admit they are wrong. While reconciliation depends on the offender, forgiveness depends on the one who was offended.

One way we can become more forgiving is by remembering to suspend judgment of our neighbors. In his book *Following Christ: The Parable of the Divers and More Good News*, Stephen E. Robinson relates the following experience he had in learning not to judge others harshly:

> Many years ago, when I was somewhere between nine and eleven, I participated in a community summer recreation program in the town where I grew up. I remember in particular a diving competition for the different age groups held at the community swimming pool. Some of the wealthier kids in our area had their own pools with diving boards, and they were pretty good amateur divers. But there was one kid my age from the less affluent part of town who didn't have his own pool. What he had was raw courage. While the rest of us did our crisp little swan dives, back dives, and jackknives, being ever so careful to arch our backs and point our toes, this young man attempted back flips, one-and-a-halfs, doubles, and so on. But, oh, he was sloppy. He seldom kept his feet together, he never pointed his toes, and he usually missed his vertical entry. The rest of us observed with smug satisfaction as the judges held up their scorecards that he consistently got lower marks than we did with our safe and simple dives, and we congratulated ourselves that we were actually the better divers. "He is all heart and no finesse," we told ourselves. "After all, *we* keep *our* feet together and point *our* toes."

The announcement of the winners was a great shock to us, for the brave young lad with the flips had apparently beaten us all. However, I had kept rough track of the scores in my head, and I knew with the arrogance of limited information that the math didn't add up. I had consistently outscored the boy with the flips. And so, certain that an injustice was being perpetrated, I stormed the scorer's table and demanded an explanation. "Degree of difficulty," the scorer replied matter-of-factly as he looked me in the eye. "Sure, you had better form, but he did harder dives. When you factor in the degree of difficulty, he beat you hands down, kid." Until that moment I hadn't known that some dives were awarded "extra credit" because of their greater difficulty.

Whenever I am tempted to feel superior to other Saints, the parable of the divers comes to my mind, and I repent . . . [H]ere in mortality, we cannot always tell who is carrying what burdens: limited intelligence, chemical depression, compulsive behaviors, learning disabilities, dysfunctional or abusive family background, poor health, physical or psychological handicaps—no one chooses these things. So I must not judge my brothers and sisters.[140]

One message we can take from Revelation 12 is this: we mustn't be an "accuser of our brethren" (see verse 10), as Satan was in the pre-earth life and as he is now.

**AN APPLICATION**

*How often do you accuse or judge others? Are you quick to forgive when others don't measure up to your expectations for them?*

We see clearly in Revelation 12 that the battle lines were drawn before the days of Adam and Eve. Notice that those who overcame Satan in the pre-earth life did so, "by the blood of the Lamb, and by the word of their testimony" (Rev. 12:11). A testimony was an invaluable weapon in the war in heaven, and it is an indispensable weapon here on Earth. Each of us had a degree of testimony in our pre-earth life, and we can resist Satan and awaken that testimony again today. As the forces of evil have

---

140 *Following Christ: The Parable of the Divers and More Good News* (Salt Lake City: Deseret Book, 1995), 34–38.

intensified and united under the influences of Satan in the latter days, the forces of good are strengthened each day by the blood of the Lamb and through the Saints' strengthening and sharing of their testimonies.

We must focus on strengthening our testimonies rather than dwelling on problems or fretting about oppositions from the adversary.

In Proverbs 4:25–27 we learn, "Let thine eyes look right on, and let thine eyelids look straight before thee. Ponder the path of thy feet, and let all thy ways be established. Turn not to the right hand nor to the left: remove thy foot from evil." The following analogy may help illustrate where we should choose to place our focus and in whom to trust: In football, the defense's goal is to get to the quarterback. Defensive linemen run and tug and fight and claw and push, all in an effort to get to the quarterback. They will continue to fight until the quarterback gives the ball to the running back; at that point, the defense shifts its focus from the quarterback to getting to the running back. In other words, once the ball is handed off, change happens. Too often in life, we metaphorically run around with our ball of problems and we won't give them up. We complain and run around shouting that life is hard and that everyone and everything is against us. If we will just give the ball of problems that we have tucked under our arm to the Lord, He will fight our battles (Ex. 14:14; Deut. 1:30).

And then what? What should we do with our testimonies and our time while trusting in God? He will surely fight the battles we are powerless to win on our own, but that doesn't mean we can step back and expect a certain desired outcome without any effort on our part. Elder M. Russell Ballard said, "We need to remember Edmund Burke's statement: 'The only thing necessary for the triumph of evil is for good men to do nothing.'"[141] We as Latter-day Saints need to be active in building the kingdom of God on the earth, overcoming the adversary with the power of our testimonies. During his address at the BYU Education Week devotional on August 19, 2014, Elder David A. Bednar urged Church members to do one simple thing to share their testimony:

> [W]hat has been accomplished thus far in this dispensation communicating gospel messages through social media channels is a good beginning—but only a small trickle. I now extend to you the invitation to help transform the

---

141 M. Russell Ballard, "Let Our Voices Be Heard," *Ensign*, Nov. 2003. Edmund Burke quotation attributed in John Bartlett, comp., *Familiar Quotations,* 15th edition (Boston: Little, Brown & Co., 1980), ix.

trickle into a flood. Beginning at this place on this day, I exhort you to sweep the earth with messages filled with righteousness and truth—messages that are authentic, edifying, and praiseworthy—and literally to sweep the earth as with a flood.[142]

Just as we each overcame Lucifer "by the word of [our] testimony" (Rev. 12:11) in the pre-earth state, one small way that we can apply a principle from Revelation 12 is to overcome demonic forces by letting our voices be heard in our day.

**AN APPLICATION**

*How often do you share your testimony? Do you find ways to testify and let your voice be heard through social media and other means?*

---

142 David A. Bednar, "To Sweep the Earth as with a Flood" (*BYU Education Week*, Aug. 19, 2014).

# *Revelation 13*
## SATAN'S KINGDOM, PART I

IN REVELATION 13:1, JOHN SAW "a beast . . . having seven heads and ten horns," that came from the sea with power over earthly kingdoms; this beast made war with the Saints and overcame them during the Great Apostasy (Rev. 13:2–11, Dan. 7:2–3).[143] The beast's many heads, crowns, and horns suggest many different kingdoms and rulers with great power. The first three animals are a lion (most likely the Babylonian Empire), a bear (a most likely the Medo-Persian Empire), and a leopard (most likely the Greek Empire). It is probable that the final world empire will have the authority of a lion, the crushing power of a bear, and the catlike speed of a leopard. The fourth animal seems to be nearly indescribable, yet represents the final world empire under the leadership of a Satanic dictator (Dan. 7:7–8). Joseph Smith taught, "When God made use of the figure of a beast in visions to the prophets He did it to represent those kingdoms which had degenerated and become corrupt, savage and beast-like in their dispositions, even the degenerate kingdoms of the wicked world."[144]

In Revelation 13, the beast:

- Had power over many nations (verses 1, 7)
- Opposed God and blasphemed against Him (verses 5–6)

---

143 The Joseph Smith Translation indicates that the beast is "in the likeness of the kingdoms of the earth" (Rev. 13:1, footnote a). This likeness to Satan is just one of the things that identifies this beast with the one popularly known as the anti-Christ. The word *anti-Christ* only appears in the Bible five times in four verses (1 John 2:18, 2:22, 4:3; 2 John 1:7). There are many names given to the anti-Christ. He is known as the little horn (Dan. 7:8), the king of fierce countenance (Dan. 8:23), the prince that shall come (Dan. 9:26), the one who comes in his own name (John 5:43), the son of perdition or the man of sin (2 Thes. 2:3). The prefix *anti-* can mean *the opposite of* or *instead of*. Hence, *anti-Christ* may mean *opposite of Jesus* or *instead of Jesus*.
144 *History of the Church*, vol. 5, 341.

- Had power like that of predatory animals over their prey (verse 2)
- Had its power from Satan (verses 2, 4)
- Was worshipped (verse 4)
- Was able to overpower many, including some of the Saints (verse 7)

The Prophet Joseph clarified, "It is not very essential for the elders to have knowledge in relation to the meaning of beasts, and heads and horns, and other figures made use of in the revelations."[145] Yet, it is interesting to note that this second beast "had two horns like a lamb" but "spake as a dragon" (Rev. 13:11). The Lamb represents the only begotten Son of God, Jesus Christ. Why would Satan appear "like a lamb"? President James E. Faust explained:

> Satan is the greatest imitator, the master deceiver, the arch counterfeiter, and the greatest forger ever in the history of the world. He comes into our lives as a thief in the night. His disguise is so perfect that it is hard to recognize him or his methods.[146]

In the Bible Dictionary under *Devil*, we read, "One of the major techniques of the devil is to cause human beings to think they are following God's ways, when in reality they are deceived by the devil to follow other paths."

John next saw a second beast, which unleashes evil by working many miracles that deceive much of mankind.[147] As the Book of Mormon teaches, Satan "doth hand down their plots, and their oaths, and their covenants, and their plans of awful wickedness, from generation to generation according as he can get hold upon the hearts of the children of men" (Hel. 6:30).

Notice in Revelation 13:18 that, "his number is six hundred threescore and six." The prophets have remained somewhat silent on exactly what

145 *Teachings of the Prophet Joseph Smith*, compiled by Joseph Fielding Smith (Salt Lake City: Deseret Book, 1977), 287.

146 James E. Faust, "The Devil's Throat," *Ensign* May 2003, 51; see also Matt. 7:15

147 President Ezra Taft Benson taught, "Satan is waging war against the members of the Church who have testimonies and are trying to keep the commandments. And while many of our members are remaining faithful and strong, some are wavering. Some are falling. Some are fulfilling John's prophecy that in the war with Satan, some Saints would be overcome." (Ezra Taft Benson, "The Power of the Word," *Ensign*, May 1986, 79).

that 666 is, but it is most likely a symbol. In the Hebrew language, there are no superlatives. There's no *tallest, shortest, highest,* or *lowest.* The way that they create superlatives is to repeat the same word three times. The number seven represented perfection. So six, being one short of perfection, when repeated three times, may be saying that the beast is the most evil, most vile, and most wicked of creatures. More on the significance of numbers will be discussed in the *Symbolism of Numbers* section.

The wicked followers of this beast are sealed in their foreheads to mark their allegiance (Rev. 13:11–18). They who worship the beast "receive a mark in their right hand, or in their foreheads" (Rev. 13:16). This may symbolize evil actions (hands) and evil beliefs (heads).[148]

The Greek term for *mark* is *charagma,* which denotes a stamp, etching, engraving, or impression. It also describes the brand a master places upon an animal or a slave. The word's most important connotation, however, may be that it describes the mark left by a serpent's bite.

In what ways do Satan's followers mark themselves? Isaiah 3:9 reads, "The shew of their countenance doth witness against them; and they declare their sin as Sodom, they hide it not. Woe unto their soul! for they have rewarded evil unto themselves." Alma 34:35 reminds us, "For behold, if ye have procrastinated the day of your repentance even until death, behold, ye have become subjected to the spirit of the devil, and he doth seal you his; therefore, the Spirit of the Lord hath withdrawn from you, and hath no place in you, and the devil hath all power over you; and this is the final state of the wicked."

What can we do to receive the Lord's mark or seal? Mosiah 5:12 teaches:

> I say unto you, I would that ye should remember to retain
> the name written always in your hearts, that ye are not
> found on the left hand of God, but that ye hear and know
> the voice by which ye shall be called, and also, the name
> by which he shall call you.

One of the ways we can remember the name by which we are called is to choose wisely when adorning our personal temples—our bodies. Prophets of God have continually counseled His children regarding

---

148 The *mark* of the dragon "in [the] right hand" (Rev. 13:16) stands in contrast to and is the converse of the *seal* placed upon the foreheads of the faithful followers of Christ (Rev. 7:3).

outward appearances. When we are well groomed and modestly dressed, we invite the companionship of the Spirit and we can be a better influence on others. As *True to the Faith* teaches:

> Your clothing expresses who you are. It sends messages about you, and it influences the way you and others act. When you are well groomed and modestly dressed, you can invite the companionship of the Spirit and exercise a good influence on those around you.[149]

Another way we can remember our Savior is by reflecting our true identites in the way we adorn another temple—our homes. President Spencer W. Kimball advised parents in this manner:

> It would be a fine thing if . . . parents would have in every bedroom in their house a picture of the temple so [their children] from the time [they are] infant[s] could look at the picture every day [until] it becomes a part of [their lives]. When [they reach] the age that [they need] to make [the] very important decision [concerning going to the temple], it will have already been made.[150]

## AN APPLICATION

*Have you marked your life with indications of Christianity? Do pictures of temples and the Savior adorn your home? Does your conversation and your appearance show the marks of being a faithful follower of the Savior?*

---

149 "Modesty" in *True to the Faith* (Salt Lake City: The Church of Jesus Christ of Latter-day Saints, 2004), 107.
150 Thomas S. Monson, "The Holy Temple—a Beacon to the World," *Ensign*, Apr. 2011.

*Revelation 14*
## THE VICTORY

HAVING BEEN SHOWN SATAN'S POWER on earth in Revelation 12–13, John is now shown the power that will overthrow it in Revelation 14. We learned from Revelation 13:5–7 that the beast reigned 42 months (three-and-one-half years) to make war with the Saints and to overcome them.[151]

Directly following this tribulation period, Christ will come with His elect to Mount Zion to execute judgment (Rev. 14:1, 15–16). John saw Christ as a Lamb on Mount Zion with others cloaked with Christlike attributes:

> These are they which were not defiled with women . . . These are they which follow the Lamb whithersoever he goeth. These were redeemed from among men . . . And in their mouth was found no guile: for they are without fault. (Rev. 14:4–5)

These also were Saints who feared and worshipped the one true God (verse 6–7), resisted the enticements of the world (verse 8), refused the mark of the beast (verse 9–11), and persevered with Christ through all that is to come (verse 12). These are great attributes of the redeemed!

Revelation 14:6 speaks of "[an] angel [flying] in the midst of heaven, having the everlasting gospel to preach unto them that dwell on the

---

151 The number 42 appears a handful of times in the scriptures and may represent a period of God's judgment. There were 42 generations each from Abraham to Christ and from David to Christ according to Luke 3:23–38 and Matt. 1:17. Notice from Matt. 1:17 that the number 42 is not mentioned specifically; rather, there are three groups of 14. Further, as we read in Rev. 11, the two prophets will preach in Jerusalem for 42 months (see Rev. 11:2). The famine in Elijah's time lasted 42 months (see Luke 4:25). Forty-two children mocked the prophet Elisha before they were killed by bears (see 2 Kgs. 2:24).

earth." President Gordon B. Hinckley revealed, "That angel has come. His name is Moroni. His is a voice speaking out of the dust, bringing another witness of the living reality of the Lord Jesus Christ."[152,153,154]

Moroni has played a major role in our faith and in the American nation. It has been reported that Moroni may have visited the Prophet Joseph Smith at least 22 times,[155] kept the golden plates safe from robbers and apostates,[156] died as a martyr,[157] helped Christopher Columbus in his voyage, inspired the founding fathers to sign the Declaration of Independence,[158] dedicated the land for the building of the Manti temple,[159] and helped design the temple garment.[160]

A favorite account of Moroni comes from the days of the Prophet Joseph Smith. In the October 2007 *Ensign*, we read:

> It began [on September 22, 1827, Heber C. Kimball] said, in the eastern horizon—a white smoke rising toward the heavens with the sound of a mighty wind. The smoke

152 President Gordon B. Hinckley, "Stay the Course—Keep the Faith," *Ensign*, Nov. 1995, 70.

153 "The angel mentioned [here] may also represent a composite of the many heavenly messengers, including Moroni, who have assisted in the latter-day Restoration of the gospel [of Jesus Christ]" (Bruce R. McConkie, *Doctrinal New Testament Commentary* vol. 3 [Salt Lake City: Bookcraft, 1990], 529–31; D&C 13, 110:11–16, 128:20–21).

154 Paris-trained sculptor Cyrus Edwin Dallin sculpted the Salt Lake Temple's angel Moroni in 1893. Cyrus was a nonmember and was simply asked to come up with an ornament for the spires. He decided on the angel Moroni after he started reading the scriptures for inspiration. He claimed, "[M]y 'angel Moroni' brought me nearer to God than anything I ever did" (Wendy Kenney, "Looking Up to Moroni," *Ensign*, Nov. 2009); J. Michael Hunter, "I Saw Another Angel Fly," *Ensign*, Jan. 2000).

155 H. Doni Peterson, "Moroni—Joseph Smith's Tutor," *Ensign*, Jan. 1992 66.

156 Jack M. Lyon, Linda Ririe Gundry, Jay A. Parry (eds.), *Best-Loved Stories of the LDS People* (Salt Lake City: Deseret Book, 1997), 39. See also *Millennial Star* No. 49, vol. XL (Dec. 9, 1878), 772.

157 Charles D. Evans, "The Fate of Moroni," *Archives Division* (Salt Lake City: Church Historical Division, 1897).

158 Orson Pratt, "Celebration of the Fourth of July," *Journal of Discourses* Jul. 4, 1854, 367–71.

159 Orson F. Whitney, *Life of Heber C. Kimball* (Salt Lake City: Kimball Family, 1888), 447.

160 Early Pioneer History: Eliza M. A. Munson, Diary by James T. S. Allred (typescript copy, *BYU Harold B. Lee Library*), 2 (see also www.allredfamily.com/james_allred5.htm, accessed Jun. 9, 2017).

moved across the sky, in the shape of a rainbow toward the western horizon. It grew wide, then bluish in color, and became completely transparent. As Heber watched with his family and several neighbors, a large, commanding army appeared, marching in platoons across the sky from east to west. "We could distinctly see the muskets, bayonets and knapsacks of the men," Heber recorded, "and also saw their officers with their swords and equipage and [heard] the clashing and jingling of their implements of war, and . . . features of the men. . . . [W]hen the foremost man stepped, every man stepped at the same time; I could hear the steps. . . .

"No man could judge of my feelings . . . it seemed as though every hair of my head was alive. This scenery we gazed upon for hours, until it began to disappear."

Brigham Young, who at that time was not acquainted with Heber, described what he had seen the same evening: "There was a great light in the East and it went to the West and it was very bright" . . . As he gazed at it with his wife, Miriam, they saw "great armies" marching across the night sky. The vision was "perfectly clear," and it remained for several hours.

Heber and Brigham and their family members who witnessed the amazing scene felt it must have been a sign from God, but they did not know its meaning. Neither Heber nor Brigham knew the Prophet Joseph Smith or that he had received the gold plates containing the Book of Mormon that same day at the Hill Cumorah, just 20 miles to the east.

The following year, Brigham Young and Miriam moved to Mendon, New York . . . less than a half mile northeast of where Heber Kimball and his wife, Vilate, lived. Brigham and Heber, just 13 days apart in age, and their wives, just 6 days apart, soon became close friends.[161]

Both families eventually met the Prophet Joseph and joined the Church.

It is not by coincidence that Moroni statues have been placed atop most every temple in the latter days. Those golden statues are a reminder of the

---

161 Marjorie H. Rice, "Living in a Chapter of History," *Ensign*, Oct. 2007.

preparatory work that Moroni is doing for the Second Coming, and that we too can prepare by looking to and living worthily of the blessings of the temple. In the opening chapter to Vaughn J. Featherstone's book, *The Incomparable Christ, Our Master and Model,* he teaches us of some of these blessings for which we can aspire:

> The season of the world before us will be like no other in the history of mankind. Satan will unleash every evil scheme, every vile perversion ever known to man in any generation. Just as this dispensation of the fulness of times brought the restoration of all that is good and holy, so also did it bring the fulness of evil. As parents, spouses, children, and members of Christ's church, we must find safety. Unfortunately, many will struggle mightily before recognizing this bitter truth: there is no safety in this world—wealth cannot provide it, enforcement agencies cannot ensure it, even membership in the Church will not guarantee it. . . . The Lord has promised: "I will go before your face. I will be on your right hand and on your left, and my Spirit shall be in your hearts, and mine angels round about you, to bear you up." (D&C 84:88.) Surely angelic attendants guard the temples of the Most High God. It is my conviction that as it was in the days of Elisha, so it will be for us: "Fear not: for they that be with us are more than they that be with them." (2 Kgs. 6:16.)
>
> Before the Savior comes the world will darken. The time will come when even the elect will begin to lose hope if they do not come often to the temples. I believe that the Saints will come to the temples not only to do vicarious work but also to find a God-given haven of peace. True and faithful Latter-day Saints the world over will long to bring their children to the temple for service and for safety.[162]

We all have been encouraged to be worthy of having a current temple recommend so we can enter the holy temple and find peace and safety. The temple (and being worthy of entering it) truly is a refuge from the world.

---

162 Vaughn J. Featherstone, *The Incomparable Christ: Our Master and Model* (Salt Lake City: Deseret Book, 1995).

## AN APPLICATION

*How often do you attend the temple? Would it be wise to arrange your schedule to go more often than you do?*

Recall in Revelation 14:4–13 the list of attributes of victorious ones who are preparing themselves for Christ's return. The victorious:

- Are not defiled with women
- Follow the Lamb
- Have no guile in their mouths
- Fear and worship God
- Resist the enticements of the world
- Persevere with Christ
- Rest from their labors

Certainly mini sermons and messages of personal application could be prepared from each of these seven attributes, but let's just focus on one. Notice that the word *rest* is associated with those who are able to overcome the enticements of the beast (Rev. 14:13). In our lives, we should seek for rest and peace and meditative moments. President Joseph F. Smith taught:

> The ancient prophets speak of "entering into God's rest" . . . what does it mean? To my mind, it means entering into the knowledge and love of God, having faith in his purpose and in his plan, to such an extent that we know we are right, and that we are not hunting for something else. . . . The man who has reached that degree of faith in God that all doubt and fear have been cast from him, he has entered into "God's rest," . . . rest from doubt, from fear, from apprehension of danger, rest from the religious turmoil of the world.[163]

Most of us try to travel the shortest path from point **A** to point **B** to gain the most in the least amount of time. In other words, our thought process tends to be, *How much can I accomplish in the least amount of time?* Speed, however, leads to the death of curiosity; wonder and awe are lost

---

163 Joseph F. Smith, *Gospel Doctrine* (Salt Lake City: Deseret Book, 2002), 58.

through busyness. Curious people slow down and wonder and ponder, exploring a nonlinear path; they have more questions than conclusions. It's important to remember that God created human *beings* not human *doings*. But God, in His omniscience, knew we'd be tempted to fill our time in these latter days (after all, He called it the dispensation of the *fulness of times!*).

Years ago, I went skeet shooting with three friends for the first time. I missed the first few skeet that were thrown and my friend Mike said, "Do you know why you are missing? You are aiming at the skeet." I was a bit puzzled. He said, "You need to aim just ahead of where it's traveling so that the pellets from the gun arrive at the skeet at the right time." I learned a great principle: If we are focused on what we can see, we may miss our target. If we can anticipate things just ahead of where life is right now, we'll have great success. As we continued our skeet shooting, I only missed once and hit every single skeet the rest of the afternoon. Making this principle relevant, we need to plan ahead if we will ever become successful at finding rest in our hectic lives. Teaching on the principle of slowing down, President Dieter F. Uchtdorf taught:

> Isn't it true that we often get so busy? And, sad to say, we even wear our busyness as a badge of honor, as though being busy, by itself, was an accomplishment or sign of a superior life. . . .
>
> I think of our Lord . . . I have tried to imagine Him bustling between meetings or multitasking to get a list of urgent things accomplished.
>
> I can't see it.[164]

## AN APPLICATION

*Do you* rest *from your labors? Are you* too busy?

164 Dieter F. Uchtdorf, "Of Regrets and Resolutions," *Ensign*, Nov. 2012.

## *Revelation 15*
## RIGHTEOUS REWARDS

THERE ARE TWO HARVESTS MENTIONED in the book of Revelation. The first harvest separates the righteous from the wicked (Rev. 15); the second harvest is God's judgments upon the wicked (Rev. 16). The righteous who are rewarded are described in Revelation 15:2–3 thus:

> 2. And I saw as it were a sea of glass mingled with fire: and them that had gotten the victory over the beast, and over his image, and over his mark, and over the number of his name, stand on the sea of glass, having the harps of God.
> 3. And they sing the song of Moses the servant of God, and the song of the Lamb (see also verse 4).

The phrase *Song of Moses* points our minds to Moses's day, but a personal message regarding music is also quietly underscored.[165] Music is certainly a powerful influence in our lives. The Lord highlighted the power of worthy music when He revealed to the Prophet Joseph Smith and Emma the following from Doctrine and Covenants 25:12: "For my soul delighteth in the song of the heart; yea, the song of the righteous is a prayer unto me, and it shall be answered with a blessing upon their heads." President Boyd K. Packer has said, "Some music is spiritually very destructive . . . The tempo, the sounds, and the lifestyle of those who perform it repel the Spirit. It is far more dangerous than you may suppose, for it can smother your spiritual senses."[166]

---

165 There are at least three songs that Moses wrote. One was sung after the crossing of the Red Sea as recorded in Exodus 15, one is recorded in Psalm 90, and the other was written in the last days of Moses's life, as recorded in Deuteronomy 32.

166 Boyd K. Packer, "Personal Revelation: The Gift, the Test, and the Promise," *Ensign*, Nov. 1994.

## AN APPLICATION

*Do you watch and listen to good media? How has your life been influenced by music?*

Seven angels, clothed with pure white linen and with golden girdles, receive from one of the four living creatures seven golden vials filled with the wrath of God. John saw the temple filled with smoke from God's power and glory so that no one could enter the temple until the seven plagues of the seven angels were completed (see Rev. 15:7–8).[167] These angels may have been preparing a sacrifice to the Lord, called *the supper of the great God*, which we will study in Revelation 19.

---

167 This description evokes the scene in the desert after the Exodus, when Moses could not enter the tabernacle because the glory of the Lord had filled it (see Ex. 40:35). 1 Kings 8 details the dedication of Solomon's temple, which resulted in the filling of the temple with the glory of God such that the priests could not enter it.

# *Revelation 16*
## WRATH OF GOD AND THE BATTLE OF ARMAGEDDON

THE EVENTS OF REVELATION 16 through 18 teach us that the vials full of God's wrath (His divine judgment) will be poured out upon the wicked, while the righteous are with the Savior in heaven. The plagues of God, as found in Revelation 16, are as follows:

First Plague
- A sore comes upon the wicked (Rev. 16:2).

Second Plague
- The sea becomes as blood (Rev. 16:3).

Third Plague
- Fresh waters become as blood (Rev. 16:4–7).

Fourth Plague
- The sun scorches men with great heat (Rev. 16:8–9).

Fifth Plague
- The beast's kingdom fills with darkness, and men gnaw their tongues and blaspheme God because of their pain and sores (Rev. 16:10–11).

Sixth Plague
- Three great evil spirits influence men to battle during Armageddon (Rev. 16:12–16).

Seventh Plague
- A great earthquake, hail, and destruction occur (Rev. 16:17–21).

The Old Testament prophet Joel saw many of the events specific to the first five plagues as envisioned by John. In Joel, we read, "And I will shew wonders in the heavens and in the earth, blood, and fire, and pillars of smoke. The sun shall be turned into darkness, and the moon into blood, before the great and the terrible day of the LORD come" (Joel 2:30–31;

see verses 28–32). When the angel Moroni first visited Joseph Smith, he "quoted the second chapter of Joel, from the twenty-eighth verse to the last. He also said that *this was not yet fulfilled, but was soon to be*" (JS—H 1:41). In the October 2001 general conference, President Gordon B. Hinckley announced, "The vision of Joel has been fulfilled."[168]

During the sixth plague, we learn that armies will "[gather] . . . into a place called in the Hebrew tongue Armageddon" (Rev. 16:16). *Armageddon* is a compound word, originating from the Hebrew "*har Megiddo*" which means "*mountain of Megiddo.*" Megiddo is a large hill where ancient forts were built as a defense against other nations and is located to the east of the Plains of Jezreel (just south of Galilee in what was originally Judea). *Megiddo* means *the place of troops.* It may have been where Josiah was killed by Pharaoh Necho (2 Chr. 35:22). The final battle between end-time forces will begin here in Megiddo. Elder Bruce R. McConkie explains that "Armageddon will be a holy war. There will be political overtones, of course. Wars are fought by nations, which are political entities. But the underlying causes and the moving power in the hearts of men will be their views on religious issues."[169]

During the battle, a plague will strike the army, causing terrible disease (Zech. 14:12; D&C 29:18–20). Only one-sixth of the invading army will survive (Ezek. 39:2). A terrible earthquake will shake the land (Rev. 11:13, 16:18; Ezek. 38:19–20; Hag. 2:6–7). A spring in Jerusalem will form a new river and the Dead Sea will have its waters healed.[170] The battle of Armageddon will be massive with the soldiers totaling 200,000,000 (Rev. 9:16). All nations will be gathered against Jerusalem to battle (Zech. 11–14). It will take seven years to burn the weapons used in this battle of Armageddon and seven months to bury the dead once the battle is over (Ezek. 39:9–12).

Zechariah 14:4–5 records that while the battle is raging and the contestants are waging war, "[H]is feet shall stand in that day upon the mount of Olives . . . and the mount of Olives shall cleave in the midst thereof toward the east and toward the west, and there shall be a very great valley . . . And ye shall flee to the valley." The Savior will create an escape route when He stands on the Mount of Olives; half of the mountain shall remove to the north, half of it toward the south.

168 Gordon B. Hinckley, "Living in the Fullness of Times," *Ensign*, Nov. 2001.
169 Bruce R. McConkie, *The Millennial Messiah: The Second Coming of the Son of Man* (Salt Lake City: Deseret Book, 1982), 477.
170 Ezek. 47:6–12; *Teachings of the Prophet Joseph Smith*, compiled by Joseph Fielding Smith (Salt Lake City: Deseret Book, 1977), 286.

Doctrine and Covenants 45 adds to the events of the prophecy:

51. And then shall the Jews look upon me and say: What are these wounds in thine hands and in thy feet?
52. Then shall they know that I am the Lord; for I will say unto them: These wounds are the wounds with which I was wounded in the house of my friends. I am he who was lifted up. I am Jesus Christ that was crucified. I am the Son of God. (See also verse 53)

Finally, those of the Jewish faith will believe that Jesus is the Christ; that the man, that great prophet, that great teacher who came 2,000 years ago literally was the Son of God. Ezekiel 39:22 reads, "So the house of Israel shall know that I am the LORD their God from that day forward." If a person was not invited to the gathering at Adam-ondi-Ahman, imagine him or her being a missionary at the Mount of Olives; that surely would be next on a righteous person's wish list! It would be quite the experience watching those from Judah finally accept Jesus as the Christ.

During the seventh plague, Revelation 16:21 describes "a great hail out of heaven, every stone about the weight of a talent: and men blasphemed God because of the plague of the hail; for the plague thereof was exceeding great." Certainly there will be no hiding places as this storm is unleashed. It is difficult for us to conceive of hailstones of this size or of the devastating effect they will have on the land (or upon the people they hit).[171] One talent weighs 76 pounds; a hailstone of that weight would be approximately 20 inches in diameter and would travel at a speed of more than 300 mph.[172] Consider this: How many crops will be left after the storm? Will water supplies still be available? "[I]t is a false idea that the Saints will escape all the judgments, whilst the wicked suffer," taught the Prophet Joseph. "[F]or all flesh is subject to suffer, and 'the righteous shall hardly escape' . . . still many of the Saints will escape . . . yet many of the righteous shall fall a prey to disease, to pestilence, etc., by reason of the weakness of the flesh, and yet be saved in the kingdom of God."[173]

---

171 The largest hailstone discovered in the U.S. fell in Vivian, South Dakota in Jul. 2010. The roughly volleyball-sized hailstone weighed 1.9375 lbs. and measured 8 inches in diameter ("Record Setting Hail Event in Vivian South Dakota on Jul. 23, 2010," *National Weather Service*, accessed Jun. 9, 2017, https://www.weather.gov/abr/vivianhailstone).

172 "The Biblical Hailstone," *Search for Noah's Ark*, accessed Jun. 9, 2017, http://www.arksearch.com:80/nahstone.htm.

173 "The Second Coming and the Millennium," *Teachings of Presidents of the Church: Joseph Smith* (Salt Lake City: The Church of Jesus Christ of Latter-day Saints, 2007), 253.

The Lord admonishes us to prepare. "Behold, I come as a thief. Blessed is he that watcheth, and keepeth his garments, lest he walk naked, and they see his shame" (Rev. 16:15). We are blessed when we keep sacred our garments we receive with our temple endowment. During the Savior's earthly ministry, He invited His Apostles to remain in Jerusalem "until [they were] *endued* with power from on high" (Luke 24:49). The Old English word *endue* is the root word of our modern English word *endow*. *Endow* means *to put on something; to invest; to clothe*. It also means *to put on as a garment; to cover*. The Greek definition has two meanings; the first is *to dress or clothe or sink into a garment*. The second is from a figurative usage meaning to take on *characteristics and virtues of another*. Receiving an endowment from on high is critical to enduring the plagues of the latter days. Brigham Young wrote of the endowment: "Let me give you a definition in brief. Your endowment is, to receive all those ordinances in the house of the Lord, which are necessary for you, after you have departed this life, to enable you to walk back to the presence of the Father, passing the angels who stand as sentinels."[174] The imagery and symbolism of the blessed, endowed with garments and walking past sentinels, is beautiful.

In the August 1997 *Ensign*, we read of the experience President James E. Faust had when he was called to serve as a General Authority:

> He was asked only one question by President Harold B. Lee: "Do you wear the garments properly?" to which he answered in the affirmative. He then asked if President Lee was going to ask him about his worthiness. President Lee replied that he didn't need to, for he had learned from experience that how one wears the garment is the expression of how the individual feels about the Church and everything that relates to it. It is a measure of one's worthiness and devotion to the gospel.[175]

## AN APPLICATION

*If you have been endowed, do you remember to properly wear your temple garments? If you have not yet been endowed, does your current wardrobe contain temple-ready clothing?*

---

174 *Discourses of Brigham Young*, compiled by John A. Widtsoe (Salt Lake City: Deseret Book, 1941), 416.
175 Carlos E. Asay, "The Temple Garment," *Ensign*, Aug. 1997.

# *Revelation 17*
## SATAN'S KINGDOM, PART II

IN REVELATION 17, JOHN SAW the judgments of God poured out upon Satan's kingdom, Babylon. He described the kingdom of Babylon as a "great whore . . . with whom [people] of the earth have committed [spiritual] fornication" (Rev. 17:1–2). This kingdom is specifically titled, "MYSTERY, BABYLON THE GREAT, THE MOTHER OF HARLOTS AND ABOMINATIONS OF THE EARTH" (Rev. 17:5).

Babylon has typified wickedness for several millennia. Located on the shores of the Euphrates River, this city was founded by Nimrod, who rebelled against the Lord and authored some of the greatest evils ever to fall on humankind in constructing a tower to reach heaven (Gen. 11). In ancient days, Satan sought to make Babylon the capital of this evil operation; in modern days, spiritual Babylon is present in the form of wickedness.

The account of the establishment of ancient Babylon is found in the Old Testament. Genesis 11:1–4 reads, "And the whole earth was of one language, and of one speech. And it came to pass, as they journeyed from the east . . . they had brick for stone, and slime had they for mortar. And they said, Go to, let us build us a city and a tower, whose top may reach unto heaven; and let us make us a name." Following the great Flood, the Babylonians used stone, slime, and mortar, which was the best building technology they had in that day. With it, they felt like they didn't need God.

The parallel to Babylon in our day is clear: Use of technology throughout time was never a problem, until it began to be used in a Babylonian way (not in harmony with God's intended purposes). It appears that from the beginning of time, Satan has loved making people feel like they can use technology in place of God; from stone, slime, and mortar to iPhones, computers, and medicine today, Satan loves to persuade people to use these magnificent creations in lieu of the Creator. He lures people to think that through using and placing their confidence in their own personal stone, slime, and mortar, their own superficial spirituality is sufficient. In reality, spiritual depth comes not from a cursory study relying exclusively on modern technology to receive answers to our questions—using this method is like striving, as did the people of Babel, to reach heaven through earthly means. The tower we climb as we worship our Heavenly Father and strive toward heaven should be daily heartfelt prayer and sincere scripture study.[176]

During the seventh seal, the powerful whore spoken of in Revelation 17 will have dominion over all the earth, for, "[she] sitteth upon many waters . . . and the inhabitants of the earth have been made drunk with the wine of her fornication" (Rev. 17:1–2). Her power is impressive and far-reaching, influencing many nations (symbolized by her *sitting on many waters*).

Elder Bruce R. McConkie taught that "the underlying causes and the moving power in the hearts of men will be their views on religious issues. The grand desideratum will be whether they are for Christ and his gospel or against him and his cause."[177] Elder McConkie further taught regarding Satan's dominion across many waters:

> [A]ll of the governments of the earth are in league with the great whore in that, from time to time, they do such things as: Prohibit the worship of God; Enact laws defining religious beliefs and prescribing forms of worship; Maintain state-supported, false systems of religion; Deny freedom of religious belief to all their citizens; Impose the religious beliefs of conquerors upon conquered people; Permit the mingling of religious influence with civil government; Foster one religious society and proscribe another; Deny to men their inherent and inalienable rights; Fail to guarantee the free exercise of conscience, the right and control of property, and the protection of life;

---

176 Eric D. Richards, "Yup. We've Got Stone and Slime and Mortar . . . ," *BYU Idaho Online Instruction Community*, posted Jan. 20, 2015, onlineinstruction.ning. com/blogs/yup-we-ve-got-stone-and-slime-and-mortar.
177 Bruce R. McConkie, *The Millennial Messiah: The Second Coming of the Son of Man* (Salt Lake City: Deseret Book, 1982); 398, 477.

Enact laws which curtail the agency of man; Require the teaching of false principles in their educational systems; Deny the representatives of certain churches the right to teach their doctrines or proselyte along their people; and Fail to punish crime and protect the rights of their citizens, particularly unpopular minority groups.[178]

Latter-day Saints believe in "being subject to kings, presidents, rulers, and magistrates, in obeying, honoring, and sustaining the law" (A of F 1:12). By application, we should earnestly seek to elect officials who are honest and wise. The Church encourages its members to be informed about political issues, to vote in elections, and to respect other members of the Church, whose backgrounds and experiences may differ from their own.[179] In a letter from the First Presidency, we read, "Principles compatible with the gospel [are] found in [the platforms of all major] political parties."[180] The founding fathers of the United States established our nation and our legislative process to use Christianity as the conscience of government.[181] Because of this truth, we, as Latter-day Saint Christians should not be a silent voice. And as nations and societies and governments drift further and further away from the Lord's standards, the greater the need becomes for the people of Zion to raise their voices.

**AN APPLICATION**

*Are you active in the political process? Do you research the current issues and promote platforms harmonious with the gospel?*

---

178 Bruce R. McConkie, *Doctrinal New Testament Commentary*, 3 Volumes (Salt Lake City: Bookcraft, 1965–1973), 553–54.

179 "Political Neutrality," *Mormon Newsroom*, accessed Jun. 9, 2017, http://www.mormonnewsroom.org/official-statement/political-neutrality.

180 "First Presidency 2016 Letter Encouraging Political Participation, Voting in US" , *Mormon Newsroom*, accessed Jun. 9, 2017, www.mormonnewsroom.org/article/first-presidency-2016-letter-political-participation.

181 As people draw closer to Zion, there is less need to be ruled by political governing; the further from Zion that people drift, the more need there is for government and societal regulations.

# Revelation 18
## SATAN'S KINGDOM DESTROYED

IN REVELATION 18, AN ANGEL proclaims that Babylon is to be destroyed; her wicked supporters will mourn her loss, while the Saints flee Babylon. Herein, this angel uses three voices in making invitations to flee Babylon.

The first voice heard is the voice of *judgment*: "I saw another angel come down from heaven, having great power . . . And he cried mightily with a strong voice, saying, Babylon the great is fallen, is fallen" (Rev. 18:1–2).

The second voice heard is the voice of *separation*: "And, I heard another voice from heaven, saying, Come out of her, my people, that ye be not partakers of her sins, and that ye receive not of her plagues" (Rev. 18:4).

The third voice heard is the voice of *mourning*: "And the kings of the earth, who have committed fornication and lived deliciously with her, shall bewail her, and lament for her, when they shall see the smoke of her burning" (Rev. 18:9).

This is a beautiful principle of surrendering our will to God. When we are invited to flee Babylon—and as soon as we adopt an attitude of surrendering to that call—God endows us with power. When Lehi asked Nephi to travel 500 miles to retrieve the brass plates, Nephi's reply was, "I will go and do" (1 Ne. 3:7). As the prophet Nephi met Ishmael and invited him to travel with him and his family in the desert, Ishmael chose to pack up his family and his life and head out with Nephi, traveling for eight years. Adam, after being removed from the Garden of Eden, received a visit from an angel who asked him why he was offering sacrifices. Adam's response? "I know not, save the Lord commanded me" (Moses 5:6). What an attitude of submissiveness! Hebrews 11:24–25 reads:

> 24. By faith Moses, when he was come to years, refused to be called the son of Pharaoh's daughter;

25. Choosing rather to suffer affliction with the people of God, than to enjoy the pleasures of sin for a season.

To use a metaphor from my youth, I once was at a baseball game and saw a batter connect his bat solidly with the ball. It screamed toward the outfield and bumbled around in the corner of the field. The outfielder scrambled to catch up with it and in the process, the runner made it all the way home. An inside the park homerun! But then something strange happened. I saw a conversation between the infielders. The ball was then tossed to the first baseman, and I then saw the umpire clench his fist and scream, "He's out!" I didn't know what had happened. My friend leaned over and explained that the runner had missed first base and, by rule, was called out once the ball was thrown there; once the baseman stepped on the bag, he was out.

The Savior taught, "[S]eek ye *first* the kingdom of God . . . and all these things shall be added unto you" (3 Ne. 13:33). In life, if we don't seek His kingdom first, we'll eventually be called out. Even if we hustle through life and make it all the way home, if we haven't touched the bases along the way, all our other efforts aren't worth much at all.

"Turn ye unto me, saith the LORD of hosts, and I will turn unto you," reads Zechariah 1:3. Much like that which was taught in Revelation 2 with the Saints in Ephesus who had left their first love, the message now presented in Revelation 18 shows that there is a difference between turning *from* and turning *to*. We can turn *from* and still be unhappy and unfulfilled and feel unsatisfied. A person can turn *from* sin and still feel that something is missing. Turning *from* is easy, but turning *to* Christ completes the process of change. Identifying, measuring, and determining how to turn *to* Christ can be a bit challenging. The prophet Haggai invited his readers, "Consider your ways" (Hag. 1:5). Simply stated, a person knows when he or she is turning *to* Christ when he or she chooses to reprioritize and reposition the role of Christ in his or her life. The culmination of returning *to* Christ occurs when a person feels at peace and satisfied with their relationship with the Lord and what they have in their lives; they go from living a dissatisfied life to living a life of joy and contentment and they stop seeking for external satisfaction and excess.[182]

---

[182] The world rewards people at certain ages. In the U.S., for example, R-rated movies are accessible to 17-year-olds without a guardian's supervision and at age 21, drinking is legal. *Coming of age* in a gospel context might be defined as the moment a person decides to leave the world and surrender their will to the Savior. Prophets constantly invite us to come of age according to the Lord's terms rather than the world's terms.

In this chapter, John saw that the world will be changing rapidly leading up to Christ's return. President Henry B. Eyring taught:

> The spiritual strength sufficient . . . to stand firm just a few years ago will soon not be enough. Many . . . are remarkable in their spiritual maturity and in their faith. But even the best . . . are sorely tested. And the testing will become more severe. . . . [W]e must raise our sights. . . . many, far too many, say to themselves: "Well, I know I may have to repent someday, and I know that a mission and temple marriage will require big changes, but I can always take care of that when the time comes. I have a testimony. I know the scriptures. I know what it takes to repent. I'll see the bishop when it's time and I'll make the changes later. I'm only young once. For now, I'll go with the flow."
>
> Well, the flow has become a flood and soon will be a torrent. It will become a torrent of sounds and sights and sensations that invite temptation and offend the Spirit of God. Swimming back upstream to purity against the tides of the world was never easy. It is getting harder and may soon be frighteningly difficult.[183]

## AN APPLICATION

*Do you feel that you have completely surrendered and submitted your will to the Lord? Do you support any group whose teachings are contradictory to the teachings of the Church?*

The reaction of the world to the falling of Babylon will be great. Revelation 18:11 reads, "And the merchants of the earth shall weep and mourn over her; for no man buyeth their merchandise any more," and Revelation 18:23 adds, "thy merchants were the great men of the earth; for by thy sorceries were all nations deceived." Recall that the Greek word for sorcery is *pharmakeia*. Some wonder if this lamenting is tied to the cessation of drugs and the revenue it generates.

With this interpretation in mind, modern-day revelations such as the Word of Wisdom in Doctrine and Covenants 89 are good applications. We should seek to guard ourselves and our families against the prevalent

183 Henry B. Eyring, "We Must Raise our Sights," *Ensign*, Sept. 2004.

use of drugs and the legislation that is being introduced around the world to legalize many substances. Elder M. Russell Ballard shared the following insight regarding Satan's addictive traps:

> The goal of the fly fisherman is to catch trout through skillful deception. The adept fisherman studies trout behavior, weather, the water current, and the types of insects trout eat and when those insects hatch. He will often craft by hand the lures he uses. He knows these artificial insects embedded with tiny hooks need to be a perfect deception because the trout will identify even the slightest flaw and reject the fly. . . .
>
> The use of artificial lures to fool and catch a fish is an example of the way Lucifer often tempts, deceives, and tries to ensnare us.
>
> Like the fly fisherman who knows that trout are driven by hunger, Lucifer knows our "hunger," or weaknesses, and tempts us with counterfeit lures which, if taken, can cause us to be yanked from the stream of life into his unmerciful influence. And unlike a fly fisherman who catches and releases the fish unharmed back into the water, Lucifer will not voluntarily let go. His goal is to make his victims as miserable as he is.[184]

Shortly after my mother and I were baptized, she began working as a registered nurse. As a single parent, she didn't have time to cook, so we began eating more processed and fast foods. Although I was only twelve, my health began to decline. I didn't have the energy I once had. I felt tired and anxious. I gained weight. I asked my mom how I could get into better shape. Hoping for a medical response, I was a little surprised when she simply said, "Live the principles of the Word of Wisdom." I thought she would give me advice on calories and carbohydrates and fats, but her answer was exactly what I needed. For family home evening the following Monday, we reviewed Doctrine and Covenants 89 and outlined an eating and activity plan. Our lifestyle change was dramatic. We both began to feel healthier and happier. I noticed more peace in my life and more quiet promptings from the Holy Ghost.[185]

---

184 M. Russell Ballard, "O That Cunning Plan of the Evil One," *Ensign*, Nov. 2010.
185 Eric D. Richards in "Run and Not be Weary," *Ensign*, Jun. 2009.

## AN APPLICATION

*Do you live the Word of Wisdom?*

In Revelation 18, we learn this principle: The Lord wants us to surrender our will to Him. This submission happens as we choose to flee Babylon. There is so much Babylonian temptation in our world with music, TV shows, movies, and the Internet. They can be fun and very titillating, but we must flee Babylon and be ready for Christ's appearance during the third woe, His appearance to the world, which we will discuss as we study Revelation 19.

# *Revelation 19*
## The Third Woe: The Lord's Appearance to the World

This chapter is one of the most dramatic in the Bible. In it, the Church, symbolized as a bride of Christ, is the guest of honor at the marriage of the Lamb in heaven (Rev. 19:1–10) and she returns with Christ during His triumphal Second Coming (verses 11–21). It is the only chapter in the New Testament where the word *Alleluia* is found, and it appears four times. His appearance to the world is described in Revelation 19:11–13:

> 11. And I saw heaven opened, and behold a white horse; and he that sat upon him was called Faithful and True, and in righteousness he doth judge and make war.
> 12. His eyes were as a flame of fire, and on his head were many crowns; and he had a name written, that no man knew, but himself.
> 13. And he was clothed with a vesture dipped in blood: and his name is called The Word of God.

Look at the contrasts: The apostate church is called a whore; the true church is a beautiful and pure bride. The harlot lives in the wilderness; the bride is in heaven. The harlot is adorned by Satan, the bride by Christ. The harlot is stained by the blood of martyrs; the bride is redeemed by the blood of our Savior. Since *atonement* means *to cover*,[186] this harlot and her inclinations toward nakedness denote her rejection of Christ and His Atonement.

Let's talk about the horse that the Savior will ride as He makes His appearance to the world. Recall that during the last week of his life, Jesus loosened and then rode a donkey into Jerusalem. Donkeys are symbols of peace and are slow in speed compared to horses. We must remember that ascension takes time; we should beware of gospel shortcuts, knowing that our own spiritual ascension will be more like a ride on a donkey than a ride on a horse.

---

186 Russell M. Nelson, "The Atonement," *Ensign*, Nov. 1996.

By way of application to our lives, yes, He will *loose* us (Matt. 21:2)—meaning He will help us become free of addictions or pains—but just as He did to the donkey, He will saddle us up as well. Why? It might be because the Savior rarely frees us just so we can be free; we are typically freed so that so we can better serve our fellow man. As a second application, picture the scene of praise that Jesus was receiving on this occasion. The onlookers publicly celebrated Jesus as the Messiah. By chance, did the donkey ever think that the crowd was celebrating her and not the Savior who was riding her? In other words, when people praise you or compliment you, don't fall into the trap of thinking that praises and accolades are going to you: the compliment is meant for the One who freed you and who is *riding* with you! Let Him *saddle you up* and let Him *take the reins* of your life! Let Him guide you. And when people compliment you or acknowledge your accomplishments or praise you, just remind them of the true source of your success: the Savior Jesus Christ who set you free.

## AN APPLICATION

*Do you give credit to God when people compliment you or your family?*

When reading of this event and seeing that the Lord uses the imagery of a marriage supper with regard to His return, our minds are thus drawn to the parable of the ten virgins in Matthew 25. Here we learn that five of these women are wise and have sufficient oil and five are unprepared and have insufficient supplies of oil. This parable teaches that many (half, it appears) will not be prepared for the return of our Savior. The oil is a symbol of preparation. Doctrine and Covenants 45:57 shares this insight:

> For they that are wise and have received the truth, and have taken the Holy Spirit for their guide, and have not been deceived—verily I say unto you, they shall not be hewn down and cast into the fire, but shall abide the day.

Having the companionship of the Spirit, contingent upon the choices we make, is a key indicator of preparation. Indeed, the oil of our lifestyles will help us know if we are ready for the Messiah's advent. Our oil is really an indication of true conversion. Only five of the ten virgins were deeply rooted and converted completely to Christ's gospel. As Elder David A. Bednar said, "[A] testimony is personal knowledge of spiritual truth obtained by revelation. A testimony is a gift from God and is available to all of His children. . . . Conversion is an offering of self . . . to God in gratitude for the gift of testimony. Knowing that the gospel is true is the essence of a testimony. Consistently being true to the gospel is the essence of conversion."[187]

Much like conversion is a gift that provides us protection from deception, a second kind of oil provides a protective blessing so that we can remain converted. Anointing is an ancient practice of shepherds. To prevent lice and other insects from inhabiting sheep's wool and burrowing into their ears (this could kill the sheep), shepherds would protect the sheep by anointing their heads with oil to make the wool slippery and impossible for insects to get near the ears. Just as the oil from the ten virgins symbolizes preparedness, anointing oil symbolizes a blessing of protection against spiritual threats.[188]

**AN APPLICATION**

*Do you actively seek for conversion through the Holy Ghost?*

Joseph Smith asks about the Second Coming, "But what will the world do? They will say it is a planet, a comet, &c.; But the Son of Man . . . which will be as the light of the morning cometh out of the east."[189] The east is significant. In the Garden of Eden, cherubim were stationed on the east side of the Garden after Adam and Eve were banished. In Exodus, the tabernacle's entrance faced east. In Ezekiel's vision, God's glory comes from the east. In our day, temples typically face east, as do graves. Why? Because of this passage in Revelation that teaches us that Christ will come from the East at His Second Coming. Traveling from east to west is anciently symbolic of returning to God.[190]

---

187 David A. Bednar, "Converted Unto the Lord," *Ensign*, Nov. 2012.

188 James W. Huntley, *Lordship vs Discipleship* (Bloomington: AuthorHouse, 2013), 143; James Rasbeary, "The Sheep and the Anointing of Oil," *Lighthouse Keeper*, accessed Jun. 9, 2017, https://broraz.com/2012/04/17/article-the-sheep-and-the-anointing-of-oil/.

189 *History of the Church*, vol. 5, 337.

190 "In Chinese Buddhism, the West represents movement toward the Buddha or enlightenment . . . The ancient Aztecs believed that the West was the realm of the great goddess of water, mist, and maize. In Ancient Egypt, the West was considered to be the portal to the netherworld . . . In Judaism, west is seen to be toward the Shekinah (presence) of God, as in [Biblical] history the Tabernacle and subsequent Jerusalem Temple faced east, with God's Presence in the Holy of Holies up the steps to the west . . . the Israelites crossed the Jordan River westward into the promised land [see Josh. 1:4]" ("West," *Wikipedia*, accessed Jun. 9, 2017, https://en.wikipedia.org/wiki/West).

Elder Charles W. Penrose describes Christ's appearance to the world thus:

> He comes! The earth shakes, and the tall mountains tremble; the mighty deep rolls back to the north as in fear, and the rent skies glow like molten brass. He comes! The dead Saints burst forth from their tombs, and "those who are alive and remain" are "caught up" with them to meet him. The ungodly rush to hide themselves from his presence, and call upon the quivering rocks to cover them. He comes! . . . The breath of his lips strikes death to the wicked. His glory is a consuming fire. The proud and rebellious are as stubble . . . Satan and his dark hosts are taken and bound—the prince . . . has lost his dominion, for He whose right it is to reign has come, and "the kingdoms of this world have become the kingdoms of our Lord and of his Christ."[191]

When He makes His appearance, there will be a day and a night and a day without darkness (Zech. 14:6–7); the Lord will be clothed in red apparel (D&C 133:48); those who have laughed and mocked the Savior's coming will realize their error (D&C 45:49–50); and the wicked will weep, wail, gnash their teeth and wish for the mountains to fall upon them (see D&C 29:15; Isaiah 2:19, 21; Alma 12:14).

A promise to the faithful and converted is that they will not be on the earth when the flames are ablaze. Jesus taught, "Immediately after the tribulation of those days shall the sun be darkened . . . And then shall appear the sign of the Son of man in heaven . . . And he shall send his angels with a great sound of a trumpet, and they shall gather together his elect" (Matt. 24:29–31). Modern revelation adds, "But before the arm of the Lord shall fall, an angel shall sound his trump, and the saints that have slept shall come forth to meet me in the cloud" (D&C 45:45). Paul in the New Testament also witnessed that "the dead in Christ shall rise first: Then we which are alive and remain shall be caught up together with them in the clouds, to meet the Lord in the air: and so shall we ever be with the Lord" (1 Thes. 4:16–17). The glory of the Savior's presence will consume the wicked (D&C 5:19; 133:41). Elder Bruce R. McConkie added:

191 Charles W. Penrose, "The Second Advent," *Millennial Star*, 1859, 21:583.

When the Lord comes in his glory, in flaming fire . . . so intense shall be the heat and so universal the burning, the very elements of which this earth is composed shall melt. The mountains, high and glorious and made of solid rock, shall melt like wax. They shall become molten and flow down into the valleys below. The very earth itself, as now constituted, shall be dissolved. All things shall burn with fervent heat. And out of it all shall come new heavens and a new earth whereon dwelleth righteousness.[192]

Who will be burned at His coming and why that method of death? Malachi 4:1 reads, "For, behold, the day cometh, that shall burn as an oven; and all the *proud*, and all *they that do wickedly*, shall be stubble" (emphases added). All those who are of a telestial state will be consumed.

According to Malachi, two groups of people will be burned. First, the *proud*, who knowingly put their will ahead of God's. In the words of C. S. Lewis, "Pride gets no pleasure out of having something, only out of having more of it than the next man. . . . It is the comparison that makes you proud, the pleasure of being above the rest."[193]

The second group that will be consumed by fire is *they that do wickedly*. The footnote to this second phrase in Malachi 4:1 reads, "Sexual Immorality." Those who are sexually impure and are not repentant are not prepared. Doctrine and Covenants 88:18 adds, "Therefore, it must needs be sanctified from all unrighteousness, that it may be prepared for the celestial glory." Everything telestial will be burned, both people and possessions.[194]

**AN APPLICATION**

*What can you do to decrease your pride and increased your virtue?*

Revelation 19:7 describes the Saints who have prepared for His return as a "wife [who] hath made herself ready." When the Lord comes again, the Saints will ready themselves through righteous living, joyfully preparing

---

192 Bruce R. McConkie, *The Millennial Messiah: The Second Coming of the Son of Man* (Salt Lake City: Deseret Book, 1982), 526–27.

193 C. S. Lewis, "The Great Sin," *Mere Christianity* (New York: Macmillan, 1952), 109–110.

194 D&C 76:103–104 teaches, "These are they who are liars, and sorcerers, and adulterers, and whoremongers, and whosoever loves and makes a lie. These are they who suffer the wrath of God on earth."

to receive Christ as a bride receives her groom. An angel invites us to "Come and gather [ourselves] together unto the supper of the great God" (Rev. 19:17). Why? A bride rarely simply puts on her wedding dress; she adorns and arrays herself with accessories to look as beautiful as she can for her groom. Elder Bruce R. McConkie taught:

> Each person called to the marriage feast will be examined separately, and of the many called to partake of the bounties of the gospel, few only will wear the robes of righteousness which must clothe every citizen in the celestial heaven.[195]

President Joseph Fielding Smith also taught about this bride-to-be:

> [A]s the bride is expected to be adorned, so also was the church. . . . until His return, when the marriage should take place . . . for hitherto she had been as Mary was with Joseph—espoused, but they had not come together, although the contract or covenant was confirmed.[196]

The marriage supper of the Lamb is the fulfillment of what was originally begun.

In a Jewish marriage, the process would begin with a contract, which was agreed to after the proposal occurred.[197] From this point on, the man and woman were legally considered as married. During the first stage of betrothal, after the contract was established, the bridegroom went away to his father's house to prepare an addition to his father's property for his wife and family to live in. Until his father gave his approval that the work was complete, the couple did not see each other. Recall that Jesus taught in

---

195 Bruce R. McConkie, *The Mortal Messiah: From Bethlehem to Calvary,* vol. 3 (Salt Lake City: Deseret Book, 1979–1981), 368.

196 Joseph Fielding Smith, "What Is Babylon?" *Times and Seasons* vol. 4, Nov. 1842–Nov. 1843, No. 20, Sept. 1, 1843, 315–16.

197 See Steve Rudd, "The Three Stage [R]itual of Bible Marriages," *Marriage in the Bible and Ancient Marriage and Jewish Wedding Customs,* accessed Jun. 10, 2017, http://www.bible.ca/marriage/ancient-jewish-three-stage-weddings-and-marriage-customs-ceremony-in-the-bible.htm; "The Jewish Wedding Analogy," *Bible Study Tools,* accessed Jun. 10, 2017, http://www.biblestudytools.com/commentaries/revelation/related-topics/the-jewish-wedding-analogy.html.

Matthew 24:36 of His Second Coming, "But of that day and hour knoweth no man, no, not the angels of heaven, but the Father only." Customarily, the Hebrew bride did not know the exact day or hour the groom would return to marry her, but only knew the general time as it drew near. "So likewise ye, when ye shall see all these things, know that it is near, even at the doors" (Matt. 24:33). The scriptures repeatedly speak of the bridegroom coming at night (likely because of the Mideast desert heat), so after the father approves of the addition to his home, the invitations go out for the wedding feast in the form of trumpets sounding and torches being lit. On the night of the marriage, the bride and her entourage would hear the trumpets and see the torches lighting the countryside and the groomsmen parading down the street. She would have to immediately arise, make a few final preparations, and then be escorted to the marriage by the wedding party.[198]

The following table summarizes this process:

| STEP | DESCRIPTION | SCRIPTURES |
|------|-------------|------------|
| **MARRIAGE COVENANT** | The groom's father pays for the bride and establishes the marriage covenant. | Acts 20:28; 1 Cor. 6:19–20; 1 Cor. 11:25; Eph. 5:25–27 |
| **BRIDAL CHAMBER PREPARED** | The groom returns to his father's house and prepares the bridal chamber. | John 6:62; John 14:2; Acts 1:9–11 |
| **BRIDE FETCHED** | At a time determined by the groom's father, the groom fetches the bride to bring her to his father's house. | John 14:3; 1 Thes. 4:13–18 |
| **BRIDE CLEANSED** | The bride undergoes ritual cleansing prior to the wedding ceremony. | 1 Cor. 3:12–15; Rev. 19:7–8 |
| **WEDDING CEREMONY** | A private wedding ceremony occurs. | Rev. 19:7 |
| **CONSUMMATION** | In the privacy of the bridal chamber, the bride and groom consummate the marriage. | Rev. 19:7 |
| **MARRIAGE FEAST** | The celebratory marriage feast occurs, to which many are invited. | Matt. 22:1–14; Matt. 25:1–13; Luke 12:36 |

198 Charles C. Ryrie, *Come Quickly, Lord Jesus* (Eugene: Harvest House Publishers, 1996), 67; Arnold G. Fruchtenbaum, *The Footsteps of Messiah*, Revised edition. (San Antonio: Ariel Ministries, 2003), 162–63.

The five wise virgins in Matthew's parable understood clearly the necessity of being prepared at all times. When the bridegroom came, they calmly arose, made some last-minute preparations, and were off to the wedding.

On my wedding day, my wife and I were sealed at 11 A.M. in the San Diego Temple. I personally did not even set my alarm clock that morning. I knew that I would wake up naturally long before our sealing and would take a shower, put on my suit, and then meet my wife at the temple. My wife, on the other hand, had a very different experience than I did that morning! Her morning began *several* hours before our sealing, at 5 A.M. Like brides everywhere, the hours leading up to our sealing were spent primping and preparing, applying makeup, perfecting hair, making sure the dress fit exquisitely, and trying at all lengths to make herself look absolutely perfect for our wedding day (and this work on the wedding day itself was just a moment of time compared to the hours of time she had put into making our entire wedding day perfect).

As we look forward to Christ's return, we should be much like those beautiful brides, both in New Testament days and in our day, who meticulously make everything about them perfect for their grooms. We, like them, should be making preparations for the bridegroom's return; each of our days should be filled with prayer, scripture study, and service to others.

**AN APPLICATION**

*Are you actively strengthening your relationship with your spouse? Are you free from pride and immorality? Are you living up to the terms of your* marriage contract, *or* covenant, *with the Savior? Do you feel that you are dressed and ready?*

## *Revelation* 20
## THE MILLENNIUM AND FINAL JUDGMENT

"AND I SAW AN ANGEL come down from heaven," Revelation 20:1–3 reads, "having the key to the bottomless pit and a great chain in his hand. And he laid hold upon the dragon, that old serpent which is the Devil, and Satan, and bound him a thousand years, And cast him in the bottomless pit, and shut him up." Remember that the devil only has power over us to the degree that we permit him to.[199] In 1 Nephi 22:26, we are taught that "because of the righteousness of his people, Satan has no power; wherefore, he cannot be loosed for the space of many years; for he hath no power over the hearts of the people, for they dwell in righteousness, and the Holy One of Israel reigneth." President Spencer W. Kimball added, "When Satan is bound in a single home—when Satan is bound in a single life—the Millennium has already begun in that home, in that life."[200] What a sweet promise! We remember what Mormon said of Moroni, the chief captain of the Nephite armies: "[I]f all men had been, and were and ever would be, like unto Moroni, behold, the very powers of hell would have been shaken forever; yea, the devil would never have power over the hearts of the children of men" (Alma 48:17).

### AN APPLICATION
*Are you making choices in your life that bind the influence of the adversary?*

Elder Bruce R. McConkie, speaking of the Millennium, taught:

> Children will be born, grow up, marry, advance to old age, and pass through the equivalent of death. Crops will be

---

199 *Teachings of the Prophet Joseph Smith*, compiled by Joseph Fielding Smith (Salt Lake City: Deseret Book, 1977), 181.
200 Spencer W. Kimball, *The Teachings of President Spencer W. Kimball*, Edward L. Kimball (ed.), (Salt Lake City: Bookcraft, 1982), 172.

planted, harvested, and eaten; industries will be expanded, cities built, and education fostered; men will continue to care for their own needs, handle their own affairs, and enjoy the full endowment of agency . . . dwelling in peace, living without disease, and progressing as the Holy Spirit will guide, the advancement and perfection of society during the millennium will exceed anything men have supposed or expected.[201]

Elder Joseph B. Wirthlin gave further insight to one of the blessings of the millennial day: "The Lord compensates the faithful for every loss. That which is taken away from those who love the Lord will be added unto them in His own way. While it may not come at the time we desire, the faithful will know that every tear today will eventually be returned a hundredfold with tears of rejoicing and gratitude."[202] Elder Jeffrey R. Holland points our minds to the glory of that day:

I bear witness of that day when loved ones whom we knew to have disabilities in mortality will stand before us glorified and grand, breathtakingly perfect in body and mind. What a thrilling moment that will be! I do not know whether we will be happier for ourselves that we have witnessed such a miracle or happier for them that they are fully perfect and finally "free at last."[203]

President Brigham Young added, "Every man and woman . . . will be as beautiful as the angels that surround the throne of God. If you can . . . obtain the right to come up in the morning of the resurrection, you need entertain no fears that the wife will be dissatisfied with her husband, or the husband with the wife."[204]

Following are some doctrines that have been revealed regarding the Millennium.[205]

---

201 Bruce R. McConkie, *Mormon Doctrine* (Salt Lake City: Deseret Book, 1966), 496–97; Isa. 65.
202 Joseph B. Wirthlin, "Come What May, and Love It," *Ensign*, Nov. 2008.
203 Jeffrey R. Holland, "Like a Broken Vessel," *Ensign*, Nov. 2013.
204 Brigham Young, "Future State of Existence," *Journal of Discourses*, Oct. 6, 1862, 10:24.
205 "The Millennium and the Glorification of the Earth," *Doctrines of the Gospel Student Manual* (Salt Lake City: The Church of Jesus Christ of Latter-day Saints, 2000), 104–6.

- Not everyone will be members of the Church or have a knowledge of the gospel when the Millennium begins (see Micah 4:5).
- The earth will become paradisiacal and glorious after being transfigured (see D&C 63:20–21; A of F 1:10; Isa. 65:17; 2 Pet. 3:10–14).
- There will be no violence during the Millennium, from men or beasts (see D&C 101:26; Isa. 2:4, 11:6–9, 65:25).
- Earth will be home to children, who will grow up and live thereupon until they reach one hundred years of age (see Isa. 65:20; D&C 101:29–31, 63:50–51, 45:58).
- The Lord will turn to the people a pure language (see Zeph. 3:9).
- All questions will be answered (Isa. 65:20–24).
- People will be free to continue with their religions and ideas for a time, until all confess that Jesus Christ is the Savior.[206]
- Those who have been resurrected will help us correct our genealogical mistakes.[224]
- The gospel will be powerfully taught to all. There will eventually be no need to teach the first principles of the gospel because "[the people] shall all know [the Lord], from the least of them unto the greatest of them" (Jer. 31:34).[224]
- The terrestrial resurrection will occur (Mosiah 26:25–27).
- The telestial resurrection will occur (D&C 29:26–29, 76:81–85, 88:100–102).
- The resurrection for those mortals going to outer darkness will occur (Alma 12:17–18).
- The devil will be loosed for a short time after the Millennium (Rev. 20:7–8; D&C 43:31, 88:110–11).
- A final war will be fought between Michael and the devil and his followers (D&C 88:112–15; Rev. 20:7–10).

At the end of the Millennium, Satan is forever "cast into the lake of fire and brimstone" (Rev. 20:10; see also D&C 88:110–16). All who have come to Earth will stand before God to be judged, as Revelation 20:12–13 (see also verse 14) states:

12. And I saw the dead, small and great, stand before God; and the books were opened: and another book was opened, which is the

book of life: and the dead were judged out of those things which were written in the books, according to their works.

13. And the sea gave up the dead which were in it; and death and hell delivered up the dead which were in them: and they were judged every man according to their works. (See also D&C 29:26–28, 128:7–8)

Of the final judgment, Elder Neal A. Maxwell teaches, "There will be no challenge then to the justice or mercy of God."[207]

Elder Bruce R. McConkie shared this insight about the book of life:

In a real though figurative sense, the book of life is the record of the acts of men as such record is written in their own bodies. It is the record engraven on the very bones, sinews, and flesh of the mortal body. That is, every thought, word, and deed has an effect on the human body; all these leave their marks, marks which can be read by Him who is Eternal as easily as the words in a book can be read.[208]

## AN APPLICATION

*Have there been any sins in your life that should have been worked out with priesthood leaders but haven't been?*

207 Neal A. Maxwell, *That Ye May Believe* (Salt Lake City: Bookcraft, 1992), 55.
208 Bruce R. McConkie, "Book of Life," *Mormon Doctrine* (Salt Lake City: Deseret Book, 1966), 97.

*Revelation 21*
## THE EXALTED EARTH, PART I

"THIS EARTH WILL BE ROLLED back into the presence of God and crowned with celestial glory," taught the Prophet Joseph.[209] Revelation 21:1–4 gives a glimpse into what life may be like once the earth receives its paradisiacal glory and what our lives may be like in heaven:

1. And I saw a new heaven and a new earth: for the first heaven and the first earth were passed away; and there was no more sea.
2. And I John saw the holy city, new Jerusalem, coming down from God out of heaven, prepared as a bride adorned for her husband.
3. And I heard a great voice out of heaven saying, Behold, the tabernacle of God is with men, and he will dwell with them, and they shall be his people, and God himself shall be with them, and be their God.
4. And God shall wipe away all tears from their eyes; and there shall be no more death, neither sorrow, nor crying, neither shall there be any more pain: for the former things are passed away.[210]

This message of heavenly peace and comfort that only God can give surely is a favorite message with our Savior. While in mortality, we are not supposed to be comfortable too often in life. Why? So the Holy Ghost can fulfill His mission as the Comforter (if we are always living in comfort, there would be no need for the Comforter). So many times the

209 *Teachings of the Prophet Joseph Smith*, compiled by Joseph Fielding Smith (Salt Lake City: Deseret Book, 1977), 181.
210 Isaiah 65:17 teaches, "For, behold, I create new heavens and a new earth: and the former shall not be remembered, nor come into mind." It appears that the new world will be so amazing that we won't even want to remember much about the old world in which we once lived.

Savior has invited us to come to Him and enjoy the peace and rest that
He provides. Following are some scriptural examples:

- "Come unto me, all ye that labour and are heavy laden, and I will
  give you rest" (Matt. 11:28).
- "[Cast] all your care upon him; for he careth for you" (1 Pet. 5:7).
- "I will turn their mourning into joy, and will comfort them, and
  make them rejoice from their sorrow. . . . For I have satiated the
  weary soul, and I have replenished every sorrowful soul" (Jer.
  31:13, 25).
- "[We] should suffer no manner of afflictions, save it were
  swallowed up in the joy of Christ" (Alma 31:38).
- "Peace I leave with you, my peace I give unto you. . . . Let not
  your heart be troubled, neither let it be afraid" (John 14:27).

Elder Jeffrey R. Holland amplified the Lord's message that we should
not allow our hearts to be troubled or afraid when he said,

> I submit to you, that may be one of the Savior's command-
> ments that is, even in the hearts of otherwise faithful Latter-
> day Saints, almost universally disobeyed; and yet I wonder
> whether our resistance to this invitation could be any more
> grievous to the Lord's merciful heart . . . I am convinced
> that none of us can appreciate how deeply it wounds the
> loving heart of the Savior of the world when he finds that
> his people do not feel confident in his care or secure in his
> hands or trust in his commandments.[211]

Hopefully we seek for time to be alone and to be with Him. Many
people wish that there were more than 24 hours in a day—but making such
a petition is telling God that He made an error in the timetable He created
for us. Twenty-four hours in one day is enough for us to accomplish what
we need, to rest from our labors, and to commune with God.

Revelation 21:21–23 describes heaven as having "twelve gates [that]
were twelve pearls . . . and the street of the city was pure gold . . . And
the city had no need of the sun, neither of the moon, to shine in it:
for the glory of God did lighten it, and the Lamb is the light thereof."

211 Jeffrey R. Holland, "Come unto Me," *Ensign*, Apr. 1998.

When the riches of heaven are considered, the small and rather petty riches of this life pale in comparison. So many people spend their lives in search of financial gain while God has promised that faithfulness to His commandments while on Earth will bring streets paved with gold.

Brigham Young taught:

> Let them not be over-anxious for the treasures of the earth.[212]
>
> The worst fear that I have about this people is that they will get rich in this country, forget God and his people, wax fat, and kick themselves out of the Church and go to hell. This people will stand mobbing, robbing, poverty, and all manner of persecution, and be true. But my greater fear for them is that they cannot stand wealth; and yet they have to be tried with riches, for they will become the richest people on this earth.[213]

Returning to John's vision of heaven, why gold and why pearls? Of all precious materials with which to adorn the city, why these two? Well, oysters produce pearls through pain and adversity; gold requires fire to burn out impurities. These two materials are typical of those who will live in the exalted city: the exalted will have been refined over a great deal of time through adversity, even adversity caused by wealth. If you are going through your own pain or adversity, take heart, and do "not be over-anxious for the treasures of the earth." As you endure through your tribulations, you are becoming more and more prepared to live in that adorned kingdom with the Savior!

### AN APPLICATION

*Do you feel heavy laden with fear? How can you feel more peace in your life?*

---

212 B. H. Roberts, *A Comprehensive History of The Church of Jesus Christ of Latter-day Saints* vol. 3 (Salt Lake City: Deseret News Press, 1930), 347.
213 Preston Nibley, *Brigham Young: The Man and His Work,* 4th ed. (Salt Lake City: Deseret Book, 1960), 127–28.

*Revelation 22*
## THE EXALTED EARTH, PART II

REVELATION 22:1–5 DESCRIBES IN GREATER detail the exalted earth:

- And he shewed me a pure river of water of life, clear as crystal, proceeding out of the throne of God and of the Lamb.
- In the midst of the street of it, and on either side of the river, was there the tree of life, which bare twelve manner of fruits, and yielded her fruit every month: and the leaves of the tree were for the healing of the nations.
- And there shall be no more curse, but the throne of God and of the Lamb shall be in it; and his servants shall serve him.
- And they shall see his face; and his name shall be in their foreheads.
- And there shall be no night there; and they need no candle, neither light of the sun; for the Lord God giveth them light: and they shall reign for ever and ever.

Elder Bruce R. McConkie taught:

> If we keep the commandments and are true and faithful in all things, we shall inherit eternal life in our Father's kingdom. Those who attain this high state of glory and exaltation shall dwell in the presence of God. They shall see his face and converse with him mouth to mouth. They shall know him in the full sense of the word because they have become like him.[214]

---

214 Bruce R. McConkie, *The Promised Messiah: The First Coming of Christ* (Salt Lake City: Deseret Book, 1978), 578.

Elder Jeffrey R. Holland added, "Those of us who are so blessed could remember the courage of those around us who face more difficulty than we, but who remain cheerful, who do the best they can, and trust that the Bright and Morning Star will rise again for them—as surely he will do."[215]

John spoke for all true disciples when he wrote, "[C]ome, Lord Jesus" (Rev. 22:20), since those faithful are those "that love His appearing" (2 Tim. 4:8). Scoffers may mockingly ask, "Where is the promise of His coming? for since the fathers fell asleep, all things continue as they were from the beginning of creation" (2 Pet. 3:4). But things will not continue forever as they are. Jesus will return, just as Revelation predicts.

## AN APPLICATION

*Are you true and faithful in all things? How can you strive to become more like Heavenly Father and Jesus Christ?*

---

215 Jeffrey R. Holland, "This Do in Remembrance of Me," *Ensign*, Nov. 1995.

*Conclusion*

> There is a real sifting going on in the Church. It's going to become more pronounced with the passing of time . . . And those days are going to require faith and testimony and family unity, the like of which we have never had.[216]
>
> We must prepare for the great day of the Lord. This preparation must consist of more than just casual membership in the Church. [We must] be guided by personal revelation and the counsel of the living prophet, so [we] will not be deceived.[217]

The burning bush that Moses saw in the book of Exodus is a great example of how revelation works. Moses saw and noticed that the bush wasn't consumed. He wasn't impressed by the fact that a bush was burning but by the fact that the bush wasn't consumed by fire. In our own revelation, one way to know if the idea came from above is that it isn't consumed; like the bush, the righteous thought or prompting remains. When God lights a fire within (revelation through the Holy Ghost), obey those promptings. President Spencer W. Kimball taught:

> In our lives the oil of preparedness is accumulated drop by drop in righteous living. Attendance at sacrament meetings

216 Ezra Taft Benson, *The Teachings of Ezra Taft Benson* (Salt Lake City: The Church of Jesus Christ of Latter-day Saints, 1988), 107.
217 Ezra Taft Benson, "Prepare Yourself for the Great Day of the Lord," *Ensign*, May 1982.

adds oil to our lamps, drop by drop over the years. Fasting, family prayer, home teaching, control of bodily appetites, preaching the gospel, studying the scriptures—each act of dedication and obedience is a drop added to our store. Deeds of kindness, payment of offerings and tithes, chaste thoughts and actions, marriage in the covenant for eternity—these, too, contribute importantly to the oil with which we can at midnight refuel our exhausted lamps.[218]

My mother is a great example of letting the Holy Ghost be her guide and trying her best to be a valiant mother in Zion. One day, Elder Jolly and his companion, Elder Smiley (actual last names), went out tracting. My mother was getting ready for her shift at the hospital when she heard a knock on the front door.

"Hi, I'm Elder Jolly."

"And I'm Elder Smiley!"

"And we have a message about the Savior for you!"

My mom, caught off guard by the (actual) names of these missionaries—who she later found out had been on exchanges that day—simply replied, "I don't have time for this," and sent them away, shutting the door.

She'd been trying to find a good church for us to join for quite some time. In her quest, she would park in front of a random church and try to *feel* if it would be a good one to attend. After parking in front of and not feeling right about the local Presbyterian church or the Methodist church or the Church of Christ over the past few weeks, she parked in front of the Baptist church one day and felt like it would be a good one. We started attending.

The night after the missionaries came to her door, she was working with a Latter-day Saint sister named Delaine St. John. "These two missionaries from your church . . . Jolly, Happy, Friendly, Smiley, something . . . came—"

Before she could finish the sentence, Delaine said, "Did you have time to talk with them?" My mom replied that she didn't invite them in because she was getting ready for work. Delaine asked, "If I have them come back, would you please listen to them? I think it would be so good for you and your son."

---

218 Spencer W. Kimball, *Faith Precedes the Miracle* (Salt Lake City: Deseret Book, 2001), 256.

My mom, not having a good reason not to accept this invitation, replied that she would listen to their message. About a week later, the missionaries returned. Upon their arrival, she asked me to go outside, as she was worried about what their message entailed; each day they came, I would go play basketball while she received the missionary lessons.

She loved the missionaries and the lessons they presented. The one hang-up she had was the idea of prophets—latter-day Moseses, Abrahams, and Isaiahs. It didn't make sense to her.

One day she went to work early to study her scriptures (she had heard that if you read the book of Isaiah out loud God will speak to you, so she'd read from Isaiah or other books of scripture each day before work for about an hour). Her quest was to get an answer to her prayers regarding this idea of modern-day prophets. She read Amos 3:7: "Surely the Lord God will do nothing, but he revealeth his secret unto his servants the prophets." All of a sudden the idea came to her, *If God chose prophets anciently, maybe there could be prophets today.* As she thought about this idea, over the intercom came a Code Blue. In her words, a *Code Blue* is "a patient who is dying rapidly." She had a feeling this would be her patient, so she collected her belongings and reported to the trauma center.

In came the gurney. Doctors and nurses were doing chest compressions and breathing treatments and running the IVs, and everyone was scrambling as they tried to save this patient who was in cardiac arrest. As everyone did everything in their power to save this patient, my mom recalled, "I was trained for that moment. This was a Level 1 trauma, and there I was, trained for moments like this, and nothing seemed to be working—none of the drugs and treatments we were administering were helping the patient."

The clipboard for this patient, containing vital information about him and his medical condition, was on the side of the gurney. She picked it up and started looking at it and saw that the situation was more dire than she first realized. This individual had drugs and alcohol in his system that were well above the legal limits. My mom thought it may have been a case of attempted suicide.

On the top right-hand corner of the data sheet, she looked and saw this patient's date of birth; she quickly did the math and discovered that this was a twelve-year-old boy. She was shocked; she knew he was young, but she had no idea he was only twelve. At this moment, the Spirit whispered to her, *Linda, this will be the case with your son if you do not join the Church.*

She came home that night and said, "Eric, we need to talk. You're going to get baptized." She had the missionaries come back and teach me the gospel. She got baptized first and, a few months later, I was baptized as well.

Elder Jolly was twenty-six years old when he was sent from Australia to San Diego and tracted into my mother and me. I've lost contact with him over the years, but there isn't a day that goes by I don't think about him and the blessing he brought to my life through the gospel, all because he chose to be obedient to the Holy Ghost's prompting to serve a mission. There probably isn't a day that goes by that I don't thank other young men for serving missions. I am grateful for a good mom who also chose to be obedient to the Spirit.

Hold onto your families; get them ready; gather them around you, and don't be afraid to teach and preach and love them enough to help them prepare for the Second Coming. The Book of Mormon Prophet Enos was taught and raised in the "nurture and admonition of the Lord" (Enos 1:1); he knew the goodness of God and the gospel but also was admonished—or corrected—based on the same set of eternal laws and principles taught by God in His gospel.

Using *For the Strength of Youth* is a terrific way for us to teach and admonish our own children. The eighteen standards presented in this inspired pamphlet are an easy way to help assess and remind our youth about standards of living as Latter-day Saints. An easy way to review the pamphlet is to simply ask your sons and daughters about how they are living up to the standards. Consider going over these questions once a month as a stewardship interview. If you are married, each spouse could take a turn every other month for balance. Schedule the interviews and provide sufficient time to conduct them in an unhurried manner. Pray to have the Spirit and the power of discernment during the interviews. Hold them in a place that is quiet and comfortable and allows privacy. Give full and sincere attention to your children and show a genuine interest in them. Help them feel comfortable and at ease and make sure they understand why the questions are being asked. Express your love for them and let them know that what is shared will be kept confidential. Here is the compilation of questions presented in *For the Strength of Youth*:

1. Are my choices leading me toward lasting happiness?
2. What can I do to be a righteous influence on those I date?

3. How does my testimony of the gospel influence my choice of clothing?

4. How can an education benefit me and my future family?

5. How does my choice of media influence my thoughts and actions?

6. How sensitive am I to the needs and desires of my family members?

7. What kind of friend am I?

8. How can I express sincere gratitude for my blessings?

9. Am I honest in all my conversations and dealings?

10. What do the words I use say about me?

11. Does the music I listen to invite the Spirit?

12. What am I doing each day to care for my body?

13. How can I bring the power of the Atonement into my life?

14. What more can I do to keep the Sabbath day holy?

15. What opportunities do I have to serve others?

16. Do I understand why sexual purity is essential to being truly happy?

17. Do I recognize that all I have comes from the Lord?

18. Am I dependable and willing to do what I say I will do?[219]

President N. Eldon Tanner explained:

> It is important that those we interview realize that they are *spirit children of God* and that *we love them,* and *let them know that we love them* and are interested in their welfare and in helping them succeed in life. . . .
>
> Remember, the interview is based on consideration, on sympathy and love. This is so important. Let the people know we love them and are only trying to help them.[220]

The Book of Mormon, which is a representation of the events of Jesus's ministry, begins its scriptural account with a family (see 1 Ne. 1:1–6) but tragically ends with a lone man (Moro. 1, 9). What's the message here? Is it that Satan is out to destroy families? Possibly. And maybe there's another message about testimonies starting within a family and

---

219 *For the Strength of Youth* (Salt Lake City: The Church of Jesus Christ of Latter-day Saints, 2011).
220 N. Eldon Tanner, "The Blessing of Church Interviews," *Ensign,* Nov. 1978.

each individual needing to stand on their own, like Moroni, and like John the Revelator.

## AN APPLICATION

*Are you preparing your family for the Second Coming? Do you regularly hold family home evening, family scripture study, and regular stewardship interviews? If you are a grandparent, do you gather your grandkids together to teach them truth and doctrine? Are you arming your family and preparing them for Christ's coming?*

You've probably noticed by now that many of the questions for application and preparation for the Second Coming were derived from our temple recommend questions. President Russell M. Nelson explained, "The Lord would be pleased if every adult member would be worthy of—and carry—a current temple recommend. Interviews . . . for temple recommends, with [members of your bishopric and stake presidency] are precious experiences. And, in a way, they could be considered meaningful 'dress rehearsals' for that grand colloquy when you will stand before the Great Judge."[221] President Howard W. Hunter similarly expressed, "It would please the Lord if every adult member would be worthy of—and carry—a current temple recommend. The things that we must do and not do to be worthy of a temple recommend are the very things that ensure we will be happy as individuals and as families."[222]

## AN APPLICATION

*Are you worthy of a temple recommend?*

## QUESTIONS FOR REFLECTION

As this point, you may feel a bit overwhelmed with the work you feel you need to do in your life. Sometimes we doubt our self-worth. Young people, for example, are often criticized or even bullied by peers, teachers, and even parents. Many adults experience personal rejection or ruined relationships. Some people honestly worry that they are simply not good enough.

The Doctrine and Covenants reminds us, "For if you will that I give unto you a place in the celestial world, you must prepare yourselves by doing the things which I have commanded you and required of you"

---

221 Russell M. Nelson, "Prepare for the Blessings of the Temple," *Ensign*, Oct. 2010.
222 Howard W. Hunter, "Exceeding Great and Precious Promises," *Ensign*, Nov. 1994.

(D&C 78:7). Remember that the Atonement covers absolutely everything. Our Savior didn't *only* suffer for big sins and major mistakes; it doesn't matter how terrible you've been or how often you've repeated a sin, the Atonement is still for you and can still make you clean and forgiven. Never believe the vicious lie that you're not good enough to change. You absolutely are. Elder David A. Bednar said,

> We may mistakenly believe we must make the journey from good to better and become a saint all by ourselves, through sheer grit, willpower, and discipline, and with our obviously limited capacities. . . . Help from the Savior is available for the entire journey of mortality—from bad to good to better and to change our very nature.[223]

My good friend Brad Wilcox likewise taught on the help our Savior provides:

> [T]he older I get, and the more I understand this wonderful *plan of redemption,* the more I realize that in the final judgment it will *not* be the unrepentant sinner begging Jesus, "Let me stay." No, he will probably be saying, "Get me out of here!" Knowing Christ's character, I believe that if anyone is going to be begging on that occasion, it would probably be Jesus begging the unrepentant sinner, "Please, choose to stay. Please, use my Atonement—not just to be cleansed but to be changed so that you *want* to stay."[224]

As I read that quote from Brad, I thought about the Final Judgment. As we exercise our faith in Jesus Christ and become perfected in him, we can come to realize that, yes, we've incurred some troubles during mortality and experienced breakdowns or moments of particular difficulty, but our Heavenly Father sent His Son Jesus Christ to help mend us. In the end, as He opens up the book of life, because of our faith in our Savior and His Atonement, our wrongs and the wrongs of others against us will simply not be there. Our Father wants us to know that His Son's love and infinite Atonement have no boundaries.

---

223 David A. Bednar, "The Atonement and the Journey of Mortality," *Ensign*, Apr. 2012.
224 Brad Wilcox, "His Grace is Sufficient," *BYU Speeches*, Jul. 12, 2011.

I love what Elder Neal A. Maxwell said: "[T]his is a gospel of grand expectations, but God's grace is sufficient for each of us."[225] The Savior encouraged, "Yea, and as often as my people repent will I forgive them their trespasses against me" (Mosiah 26: 30).

With that knowledge of the promises associated with Christ's Atonement and the blessed forgiveness He offers, take a few minutes to review your life and get a bearing on your areas of strength—and areas that may need improvement. Below is a summary of the application principles and questions that have been asked throughout this book; the verses in Revelation examined and pertaining to those questions are included. As we review our own lives and conduct against these questions, it can be overwhelming to see how much change we need to make. But as we have seen from Elder Maxwell's and the Savior's words in the previous paragraph, as often as we repent and try to change, the Lord will forgive and help us.

- Do you have a testimony of the Atonement of Christ and of His role as Savior and Redeemer? Do you feel that the Savior is the center of your worship and of your life? (Rev. 1:8)
- Do you prepare for and strive to keep the Sabbath Day holy? (Rev. 1:10)
- Do you sustain priesthood leaders, despite their human imperfections? (Rev. 1:16–17)
- Do you feel chastened by the Spirit? (If so, it's actually a great sign that you are sensitive to the Holy Ghost; Rev. 2–3)
- Is the Savior your first and true love? Do you have any fish in your life? (Rev. 2:4)
- Is there any hypocrisy in your life? Is there anything in your actions that contradicts your covenants? (Rev. 2:9)
- How well do you prepare to take the sacrament each Sunday? (Rev. 2:17)
- Are there any temptations that you have allowed to enter into your life? Do you feel that your study of the scriptures is enough to overcome temptations? (Rev. 2:26–27)
- How well do you remember the Lord throughout each day? Do you keep a journal or a family history? Do you record the Lord's dealings within your life? (Rev. 3:3)
- How is your level of patience with others? (Rev. 3:10)

225 Neal A. Maxwell, "Notwithstanding My Weakness," *Ensign*, Nov. 1976.

- Are you seeking to obtain more and more things? Are you truly grateful and content with what you've been given? (Rev. 3:17)
- Do you actively and eagerly volunteer your time, talents, and possessions to help others? (Rev. 4:10, 5:10)
- Do you have a testimony of God, Jesus Christ, and the Holy Ghost? Is your view of the Godhead and Their characters accurate, and does it reflect what prophets have taught about the nature of the Godhead? (Rev. 5)
- How would you rate the level of purity in your life? Are you free from media that shows violent imagery? (Rev. 6:2, 4)
- How would you rate your level of temporal preparedness (e.g., food storage, disaster preparedness, savings) for the Second Coming? (Rev. 6:5)
- How are your personal prayers? Do you pray each morning before your day begins and kneel each night to pray again? (Rev. 5:8)
- Do you actively live the gospel? Do you home/visit teach each month? Are you a blessing to your ward and neighborhood? Are you a high-yield, low-maintenance Saint? (Rev. 6:9–11)
- Do you look forward to Jesus's Second Coming? If not, what can you do to become more excited about His arrival? (Rev. 6:12–17)
- Do you sustain and honor priesthood leaders? Do you sustain the President of the Church and the members of the Quorum of the Twelve Apostles? Do you sustain your stake president? Do you sustain your bishop/branch president? (Rev. 7)
- Do you keep your thoughts clean, positive, and uplifting? (Rev. 7:2–3, 14)
- Are you patient when the Lord is silent? (Rev. 8:1)
- Do you seek repentance and change often? Do you quickly follow prophetic and local priesthood counsel when it is given? (Rev. 8–9)
- Do you attend your sacrament and other meetings? How well do you prepare for this worship service? (Rev. 9)
- Are you free from media glorifying murder for entertainment purposes? Are you clean of drug abuse? Are you free from pornography? Are you free from stealing? (Rev. 9:21)
- How would you rate your personal scripture study? (Rev. 10:8–9)
- Do you have faith in God's timetable? Do you cling to hope when all seems lost or doomed? (Rev. 11:9–12)

- How often do you share your testimony? Do you find ways to testify and "let your voice be heard" through social media and other means? (Rev. 12:7–12)
- Do you ever accuse or judge others? Are you quick to forgive? (Rev. 12:10)
- Have you marked your life with indications of Christianity? Do pictures of temples and the Savior adorn your home? Do your conversations and your appearance show the marks of being a faithful follower of the Savior? (Rev. 13)
- How often do you attend the temple? Would it be wise to arrange your schedule to go more often than you do? (Rev. 14:6)
- Do you rest from your labors? Are you too busy? (Rev. 14:13)
- Do you watch and listen to good media? (Rev. 15:2–3, see also verse 4)
- If you have been endowed, do you remember to properly wear your temple garments? If you have not yet been endowed, does your current wardrobe contain temple-ready clothing? (Rev. 16:15)
- Are you active in the political process? Do you research the current issues and promote platforms harmonious with the gospel? (Rev. 17)
- Do you feel you have completely surrendered and submitted your will to the Lord's? Do you support any group whose teachings are contradictory to the teachings of the Church? (Rev. 18:1–9)
- Do you live the Word of Wisdom? (Rev. 18:23)
- Are you actively strengthening your relationship with your spouse? Are you free from pride and immorality? Are you living up to the terms of your marriage contract, or covenants? Do you feel that you are dressed and ready? (Rev. 19:7)
- Do you give credit to God when people compliment you or your family? (Rev. 19:11–13)
- Do you actively seek for conversion through the Holy Ghost? (Rev. 19:11–13)
- Are you making choices in your life that bind the influence of the adversary? (Rev. 20:1–3)
- Have there been any sins in your life that should have been worked out with priesthood leaders but haven't been? (Rev. 20:12–14)
- Do you feel heavy laden with fear? How can you feel more peace in your life?

- Are you true and faithful in all things? How can you strive to become more like Heavenly Father and Jesus Christ?
- Are you preparing your family for the Second Coming? Do you regularly hold family home evening and family scripture study and hold regular stewardship interviews? If you are a grandparent, do you gather your grandkids together to teach them truth and doctrine? (Rev. 22:6–7)

Please allow one more analogy. Each morning, after my gospel study, I watch SportsCenter on ESPN. This show provides a fun recap of the previous day's games. In typical fashion, the broadcasters will introduce the game and then highlight a few players and share a bit about the two team's rivalries, or they will share fun facts about each team's history. As the highlights begin, the producers show a team's bad plays and miscues, painting a visual picture of gloom and doom, punctuated with SportsCenter animations and sound bites. But then the mood will change. As if it almost happened miraculously, they begin to show video clips that show new developments from the game. The broadcasters begin to get excited as they commentate on the turn of events that happened during the game. Finally, and in crescendo, they then reveal the final score, knowing that they and the show's producers have edited the plays in a way so as to set up the viewers for a dramatic outcome of events.

As I watch the highlights from my favorite teams' games, I don't fall for the broadcaster's setups. I sit quietly and calmly, enjoying the video clips and highlights. Even when they speak of how poorly my team is doing, I do not get rattled. Why? At the bottom of SportsCenter's screen, they have a black scrolling bar that shows the scores of each game. Because I already know the score of the game, I am not frazzled by the commentary as I watch the highlights. In other words, the game is already over and the score has already been revealed and because of that, I am not rattled one bit (although I do quite enjoy listening to how they set up the highlight reels).

Elder Holland taught, and it's a perfect ending for our study,

> The future of this world has long been declared; the final outcome between good and evil is already known. There is absolutely no question as to who wins because the victory has already been posted on the scoreboard. The only really strange thing in all of this is that we are

still down here on the field trying to decide which team's jersey we want to wear.[226]

"Fear thou not; for I am with thee." The Lord's words, as shared by the prophet Isaiah, continue: "[B]e not dismayed; for I am thy God: I will strengthen thee; yea, I will help thee; yea, I will uphold thee" (Isa. 41:10).

My friends, square your shoulders, stand tall, and face the future with confidence, knowing He is indeed returning and that we can be prepared as we look for principles of preparation for the Second Coming as found in the revealed word of God.

---

226 Jeffrey R. Holland, email correspondence to John Bytheway, Jun. 1, 2004 (*When Times Are Tough* [Salt Lake City: Deseret Book, 2004].) in David A. Lewis, "Time to Build" (*BYU–Hawaii Devotional*, Nov. 20, 2012).

*Appendix*

## SINGLE-SENTENCE SERMONS FROM THE BOOK OF REVELATION

- "Jesus Christ . . . is the faithful witness" (Rev. 1:5).
- "[Thou] hast borne, and hast patience, and for my name's sake hast labored, and hast not fainted" (Rev. 2:3).
- "To him that overcometh will I give to eat of the tree of life" (Rev. 2:7).
- "[B]e thou faithful unto death, and I will give thee a crown of life" (Rev. 2:10).
- "[H]old fast till I come" (Rev. 2:25).
- "Because thou hast kept the word of my patience, I also will keep thee from the hour of temptation" (Rev. 3:10).
- "I would thou wert cold or hot" (Rev. 3:15).
- "As many as I love, I rebuke and chasten" (Rev. 3:19).
- "Behold, I stand at the door, and knock: if any man hear my voice, and open the door, I will come in to him, and will sup with him, and he with me" (Rev. 3:20).
- "To him that overcometh will I grant to sit with me in my throne" (Rev. 3:21).
- "I will shew thee things which must be hereafter" (Rev. 4:1).
- "Thou art worthy, O Lord, to receive glory and honour and power: for thou hast created all things" (Rev. 4:11).
- "[T]he Lion of the tribe of Juda, the Root of David, hath prevailed" (Rev. 5:5).
- "[A] great multitude, which no man could number, of all nations, and kindreds, and people, and tongues, stood before the throne, and before the Lamb, clothed with white robes" (Rev. 7:9).

- "Blessing, and glory, and wisdom, and thanksgiving, and honour, and power, and might, be unto our God for ever and ever" (Rev. 7:12).
- "They shall hunger no more, neither thirst any more; neither shall the sun light on them, nor any heat" (Rev. 7:16).
- "[T]he prayers of the saints, ascended up before God out of the angel's hand" (Rev. 8:4).
- "I took the little book . . . and ate it up; and it was in my mouth sweet as honey" (Rev. 10:10).
- "[H]e shall reign for ever and ever" (Rev. 11:15).
- "[T]hey overcame [the devil] by the blood of the Lamb, and by the word of their testimony" (Rev. 12:11).
- "Here is the patience and the faith of the saints" (Rev. 13:10).
- "[H]is Father's name [is] written in their foreheads" (Rev. 14:1).
- "I saw another angel fly in the midst of heaven, having the everlasting gospel to preach unto them that dwell on the earth, and to every nation, and kindred, and tongue, and people" (Rev. 14:6).
- "Great and marvellous are thy works, Lord God Almighty; just and true are thy ways, thou King of saints" (Rev. 15:3).
- "[T]hey that are with him are called, and chosen, and faithful" (Rev. 17:14).
- "Come out of [Babylon], my people, that ye be not partakers of her sins" (Rev. 18:4).
- "Alleluia; Salvation, and glory, and honour, and power, unto the Lord our God" (Rev. 19:1).
- "The Lord God omnipotent reigneth" (Rev. 19:6).
- "[T]he marriage of the Lamb is come, and his wife hath made herself ready" (Rev. 19:7).
- "[T]he testimony of Jesus is the spirit of prophecy" (Rev. 19:10).
- "I saw heaven opened, and behold a white horse; and he that sat upon him was called Faithful and True" (Rev. 19:11).
- "They lived and reigned with Christ a thousand years" (Rev. 20:4).
- "The dead were judged out of those things which were written in the books, according to their works" (Rev. 20:12).
- "I saw a new heaven and a new earth: for the first heaven and the first earth were passed away" (Rev. 21:1).
- "[H]e will dwell with them, and they shall be his people, and God himself shall be with them, and be their God" (Rev. 21:3).

- "God shall wipe away all tears from their eyes; and there shall be no more death, neither sorrow, nor crying, neither shall there be any more pain: for the former things are passed away" (Rev. 21:4).
- "Behold, I come quickly; and my reward is with me, to give every man according as his work shall be" (Rev. 22:12).
- "[T]he Spirit and the bride say, Come. And let him that heareth say, Come. And let him that is athirst come. And whosoever will, let him take the water of life freely" (Rev. 22:17).

## SYMBOLISM OF NUMBERS

As you've probably noticed, the book of Revelation contains many, many numbers throughout its verses. Anciently, numbers were used as symbols, full of many inner meanings; numbers (and letters) are the language for the Jewish people and are knit to their religious practices as well as their everyday habits. Elder Orson F. Whitney taught, "God teaches with symbols; it is his favorite method of teaching."[227] Similarly, Elder Bruce R. McConkie noted, "It is wholesome and proper to look for similitudes of Christ everywhere and to use them repeatedly in keeping him and his laws uppermost in our minds."[228] Christ really is the Master Teacher and He often uses His creations to teach about His Plan of Salvation and gospel principles. As we look for the symbols behind numbers found in scriptures, we will never read the scriptures the same way again.

Below is a list of a numbers along with possible symbols and stories associated with each one to help you find converting principles as you study scripture.[229]

## ONE

The number one is symbolic of the Lord, unity, and holiness. He is called *the Holy One of Israel* (see 2 Ne. 25:29). In Zechariah 14:9 we read, "There

227 Orson F. Whitney, *Improvement Era*, (Salt Lake City: The Church of Jesus Christ of Latter-day Saints, Aug. 1927), 861.
228 Bruce R. McConkie, *The Promised Messiah* (Salt Lake City: Deseret Book, 1978), 453.
229 For more information on the symbolism in numbers, see E. W. Bullinger, *Number in Scripture* (Eastfort: Martino Fine Books, 2011); John J. Davis, *Biblical Numerology* (Grand Rapids: Baker Book House, 1968); Michael L. Munk, *The Wisdom in the Hebrew Alphabet* (Brooklyn: Mesorah Publications, 1986); Friedrich Weinreb, *Roots of the Bible* (Braunton: Merlin Books, 1986); Alonzo L. Gaskill, *The Lost Language of Symbolism* (Salt Lake City: Deseret Book, 2012).

shall be one LORD, and His name one" (see verses 7–9). "The LORD our God is one LORD," reads Deuteronomy 6:4. John 10:30 adds, "I and my Father are one." The first commandment given to Moses reads, "Thou shalt have no other gods before me" (Ex. 20:3), inviting us to place God and His holiness first in our lives. When two people are married, it can be referred to as *holy matrimony* as the two become one.

## TWO

The number two is symbolic of division. Recall that there were two trees in the Garden of Eden causing division (Gen. 2:9). In the Old Testament, two birds or goats were taken for sacrifice and one was slain and one was set free (Lev. 14:4–3, 16:7–10). The Savior admonished us to not be divided by serving two masters (see Matt. 6:24). Two cherubim guarded the ark of the covenant, dividing or separating man from God (Ex. 25:18–20). Two angels were sent to Sodom (Gen. 19:1) as the Lord sought to divide the wicked from the righteous in that sinful city. Noah brought two of every kind of animal into the ark during the time when the Lord was separating the righteous followers from the wicked rebels (Gen. 6).

## THREE

The number three is typical of covenants. We make sacred covenants with all three members of the Godhead, covenanting with God in the name of Christ through the power of the Holy Ghost.[230] The tabernacle, a place of covenant-making, had three places: an outer court, the holy place, and the most holy place (Ex. 27:9–19). The ark of the covenant contained three objects: the golden pot of manna, Aaron's staff that had budded, and the stone tablets of the covenant (Heb. 9:4). There were three primary feast days in Israel as they sought to make and keep covenants with God: Passover, Pentecost, and Tabernacles (Ex. 23:14–19). The baby Moses, who would eventually receive the new covenant (the Ten Commandments) from the Lord, was placed in the river after three months (Ex. 2:3; Acts 7:20; Heb. 11:23). Esther, seeking for she and her people to establish an agreement with the Lord, said, "Go . . . and fast ye for me, and neither eat nor drink three days, night or day" (Esth. 4:16). Abraham, making a covenant with God, went to offer his only son Isaac on the third day of his journey to

---

230 *Teachings of Presidents of the Church: Joseph Smith* (Salt Lake City: The Church of Jesus Christ of Latter-day Saints, 2007), 36–44.

Moriah (Gen. 22:4–11). Samuel was called by the Lord three times (1 Sam. 3:7–10) before covenanting to serve Him. Mary, the mother of Jesus, visited Elizabeth and stayed for three months (Luke 1:56). Satan tempted Jesus three times, trying to persuade Him to break covenants (see Matt. 4:1–10). Christ prayed in three periods in Gethsemane (Matt. 26:39, 42, 44). Peter denied Christ three times (Luke 22:54–62). Recall that one-third of God's children rebelled against covenants in the pre-earth life (D&C 29:36). Noah had three sons: Shem, Ham, and Japheth (Gen. 6:10), and the Lord established a new covenant with him.[231] The ark that Noah built was three stories high and three hundred cubits long (see Gen. 6:15–16). We read in modern revelation that the three degrees of glory separate God's children based on covenants kept or broken (D&C 76).

Following are other notable uses of the number three: Elijah poured water on his burnt offering three times (1 Kgs. 18:34) and stretched himself over a dead child three times in an effort to raise the boy from the dead (1 Kgs. 17:21). Daniel and his three friends were schooled for three years with regard to the language and literature of the Babylonians (Dan. 1:3–5). Daniel prayed three times a day, giving thanks to God (Dan. 6:10, 13). Jesus served a three-year mortal ministry. On Golgotha were three crosses. Darkness reigned for some three hours while Jesus was on the cross, and there were three days of darkness in the Americas. Paul stayed in Ephesus for three months and spoke boldly in the synagogue (Acts 19:8), and subsequently stayed three months in Greece (Acts 20:3), stayed on the island of Malta for three months (Acts 28:11), and served three missions. Peter was instructed via a vision three times to eat animals previously declared to be unclean (Acts 10:9–16). The Lord talked for three hours to the brother of Jared (Ether 2:14).

## FOUR

The number four may represent things that are temporal and tied to the earth. On the fourth day of creation the world itself was finished (Gen. 1:14–19; consider also the four corners of the earth, the four seasons, and the four rivers in the Garden of Eden). Four times, Eve, the mother of all living, is mentioned in the Bible by name (Gen. 3:20; Gen. 4:1; 2 Cor. 11:3; 1 Tim. 2:13). The rain descended during the Great Flood for 40 days (Gen. 7:17). There were 400 years of bondage before Moses freed the

---

231 The Lord covenanted with Noah that He would never again cover the earth with a flood (see "Noah," *Bible Dictionary*; Gen. 9:1–17; Moses 7:49–52).

Lord's people (Gen. 15:13). There were 400 years of Apostasy between the time of Malachi and the birth of Christ (the book of Malachi was written about 432–424 B.C. and Matthew was written about A.D. 40). Remember that the children of Israel wandered for 40 years in the wilderness (Num. 32:13) and that both Jesus (Matt. 4:1–11) and Moses (Ex. 34:28) fasted for 40 days. In the parable of the sower (Matt. 13) there are four kinds of soil. While on the cross, the Roman soldiers divided up Jesus's clothes into four parts (John 19:23), pointing our minds possibly to their fixation with things temporal and forgetting the Eternal Being who hung before them on the cross.

## FIVE

The number five is a symbol for the Atonement of Jesus Christ and His grace. There were five sacrifices portrayed in Genesis 15:9 by Abraham, symbolic of the ultimate sacrifice made by Jesus Christ. Leviticus outlines five sacrifices needed for forgiveness (Lev. 1–3: burnt offering, sin offering, meal offering, trespass offering, and peace offering). The fifth time Noah's name is used is in Genesis 6:8, which reads, "But Noah found favor in the eyes of the Lord." The fifth time the name Ruth is found in the Bible, the verse (Ruth 2:2) speaks of grace: "And Ruth . . . said unto Naomi, Let me now go to the field, and glean ears of corn after him in whose sight I shall find grace." The fifth time the name Boaz is found in the Bible, the verse also speaks of grace: "Then she fell on her face, and bowed herself to the ground, and said to him, Why have I found grace in thine eyes, that thou shouldst take knowledge of me, seeing as I am a stranger?" (Ruth 2:10). The fifth time that the book of 1 Samuel 16:22 mentions David reflects a similar grace: "And Saul sent to Jesse, saying, Let David, I pray thee, stand before me; for he hath found favor in my sight." In 1 Samuel 17:40, David chooses five smooth stones to fight Goliath; we need the Atonement to fight our battles in life as well. Benjamin was honored by Joseph, who is a type and a shadow of Jesus Christ, with five times more food than his brothers (Gen. 43:34) and five sets of clothes (Gen. 45:22). The tabernacle, a place where believers went to perform ordinances pointing to the Atonement, contained five curtains (Ex. 26:3), five bars (Ex. 26:26–27), five pillars, five sockets (Ex. 26:37), and an altar made of wood that was five cubits long and five cubits wide (Ex. 27:1); the height of the court within the tabernacle was five cubits (Ex. 27:18). The number five is found 318 times in the Bible. The number 318 is significant, because it is the number of armed servants in Abram's house who rescued Lot (Gen. 14:14), just as the Atonement rescues us in our lives, reminding us that it is grace that rescues us and sets the captive free. In the Book of Mormon, Samuel the Lamanite prophesied to the people that in five years the ultimate grace of God would be manifest in the birth of the Messiah (Hel. 14:2).

## SIX

The number six is synonymous with being incomplete (and correlates to wickedness). Recall that man was created on the sixth day (Gen. 1:24–31); a day on earth consists of twenty-four hours (four times six), with twelve months in a year (two times six), hours consisting of sixty minutes (ten times six), and minutes containing sixty seconds (ten times six). In the Old Testament, Cain's descendants are given only as far as the sixth generation (Gen. 4:16–24). Hebrew slaves were to serve for six years (Ex. 21:2). Moses had to wait for six days before he was allowed to go up the mount to meet the Lord (Ex. 24:16–18). Man must wait six thousand years to meet the Lord in the Second Coming of Christ (Rev. 6:12). In Daniel 3, King Nebuchadnezzar of Babylon erected a wicked idol 60 cubits high and 6 cubits wide. Goliath was six cubits and six inches tall (1 Sam. 17:4), wearing six pieces of armor and weaponry (1 Sam. 17:5–7), including a spear whose head weighed 600 shekels of iron (1 Sam. 17:7), and was a symbol of wickedness for centuries to come. Jesus's first miracle changed six pots of water to wine for the wedding feast (John 2:6–9), teaching us that He can purify and change our wickedness into something better.

## SEVEN

In contrast with six is the number seven. Seven represents being complete, whole, and perfect. In the book of Revelation, we find seven seals, the seven stars, the seven churches, and the seven lamps (Rev. 1:20). There is a lamb with seven horns and seven eyes (Rev. 5:6); there are seven angels with seven trumpets (Rev. 8:2); seven thunders (Rev. 10:3); a dragon with seven heads (Rev. 13:1); seven angels having the seven last plagues (Rev 15:1); seven golden bowls of the wrath of God (Rev. 15:7): a scarlet-colored beast with seven heads (Rev. 17:3), which are seven mountains (Rev 17:9); and seven kings (Rev. 17:10). In Revelation, the word "Jesus" is found seven times, "Jesus Christ" seven times, and "the wrath of God" seven times. In the Old Testament, it took seven days to consecrate Aaron and his sons to the priesthood (Lev. 8:31–35). Enoch, whose city was whole and close to perfect, was said to be "the seventh from Adam" (Jude 1:14). Joshua marched for seven days with the seven priests blowing seven trumpets as they went around the walls of Jericho, and the seven-times march occurred on the seventh day (Josh. 6). Job, a *perfect* man (Job 1:1), had seven sons (Job 1:2, 42:13). Naaman washed in the Jordan seven times before becoming clean. Elisha lay upon a dead boy and after the boy sneezed seven times, he arose (2 Kgs. 4:35). An animal was required to be seven days old before it could be offered in sacrifice (Ex. 22:30). Israel was commanded to remove all leaven from their homes for a period of seven days (Ex. 12:15, 19) prior to Passover. Blood was sprinkled on the mercy seat seven times on Yom Kippur. Jesus made seven statements while on the cross. Seven churches are noted in the land of Zarahemla (Mosiah 25:23). Seven converted Lamanite cities and lands are listed (Alma 23:7–13). The Nephite monetary system was based on the number seven (Alma 11). Seven were killed by Ammon at the Waters of Sebus (Alma 18:16). Nephite tribes are numbered at seven, consisting of the "Nephites, Jacobites, Josephites, Zoramites, Lamanites, Lemuelites, and Ishmaelites" (Jacob 1:13). Think also of seven days of creation, seven notes making a perfect scale, seven gospel dispensations, seven colors of the rainbow, seven seas of the ocean, and seven continents.

**EIGHT**

The number eight relates to a new beginning. Eight souls were saved from the flood in Noah's day, which was a new beginning for humankind. The sons of Abraham were to be circumcised on the eighth day (Gen. 17:12), symbolic of a new beginning for the baby boy. In Leviticus 8:33, priests emerged from the tabernacle on the eighth day and began anew. There were eight recorded miracles performed by the great prophet Elijah. The tabernacle was dedicated in an eight-day ceremony, which was a new beginning for the children of Israel. The ancient temple's outer court had eight steps (Ezek. 40:31, 34, 37, 41), symbolic of a new beginning that came as people entered the holy edifice. David, the new king, was the eighth son of Jesse, while Solomon was the eighth son of David. Eight people were brought back to life in the scriptures. There are eight New Testament writers: Matthew, Mark, Luke, John, Paul, James, Peter, and Jude. Bethlehem, the cradle of the new beginning through Christ, is mentioned exactly eight times in the New Testament. Jesus and His Apostles were transfigured on the eighth day (Luke 9:28). From one perspective, Jesus was raised from the dead on the eighth day (Saturday is the seventh day of the week, and He rose on a Sunday), the new beginning of the First Resurrection. The eighth dispensation will be the Millennium, a new beginning. The Jaredites prepared eight barges (Ether 3:1) as they began a new life in the Americas. Nephi and his family spent eight years in the wilderness after starting their new life outside of Jerusalem (1 Ne. 17:4). Alma and his new converts traveled "eight days' journey into the wilderness" to escape King Noah and his men (Mosiah 23:3).

## NINE

The number nine is associated with posterity and judgment. Noah's generation was ninth from Adam. The Bible has nine records of stoning, nine records of blindness, and nine records of leprosy, each symbolic of judgment. There are nine fruits of the Spirit mentioned in Galatians 5:22–23; nine gifts of the Spirit in 1 Corinthians 12:8–10; and nine beatitudes in Matthew 5:3–11. Jesus, our Judge, hung on the cross until the ninth hour (Matt. 27:35–45). On a side note, human gestation lasts nine months.

## TEN

The number ten relates to divine order. Examples of this divine order include the Ten Commandments, ten plagues, ten lost tribes of Israel, and ten percent tithing. Abraham's servant brought ten camels as gifts to Rebekah, symbolic of God's orderly hand being upon the future marriage of Abraham to Rebekah (Gen. 24:10). Ten times was the name of God uttered by the high priest on the Day of Atonement (Ex. 30; Lev. 16).[232] The Passover lamb was selected on the tenth day of the month (Ex. 12:3). The tenth time Isaac is mentioned is in Genesis 22:3, in which we see his father taking him to Mount Moriah. There were ten virgins mentioned in Matthew 25 by the Master; five were wise and five were foolish (five had applied the Atonement and five may not have). The Savior taught using ten servants entrusted with ten pounds (Luke 19:13), the most capable of whom was placed over ten cities (Luke 19:17).

232 Alfred Edersheim, "The Day of Atonement," The Temple: Its Ministry and Services, accessed June 25, 2017, https://philologos.org/__eb-ttms/temple16.htm.

## TWELVE

The number twelve typifies priesthood and divine government. There are twelve foundations in the New Jerusalem (Rev. 21:14). There are twelve gates, twelve angels at the gates (Rev. 21:12), and twelve pearls at the gates (Rev. 21:21). The city is foursquare at 12,000 furlongs (Rev. 21:16). The wall is 144 cubits high (Rev. 21:17), which is 12 times 12. Revelation mentions a tree with twelve kinds of fruit twelve times a year eaten by twelve times 12,000 or the 144,000 (Rev. 21). There are twelve Apostles in the New Testament and twelve tribes of Israel and twelve Apostles today. In the Old Testament, Moses sent twelve spies into the promised land (Num. 13:1–16). There were twelve stones in the high priest's breastplate (Ex. 28:21) and twelve stones Joshua placed in the bed of Jordan (Josh. 4:8–9). Solomon had twelve officers ruling with responsibility (1 Kgs. 4:7). The baptismal font in temples rests upon the back of twelve oxen facing the four cardinal directions (1 Kgs. 7:23–26; 2 Chr. 4:3–5). When Jesus fed the 5,000 His disciples picked up twelve baskets full of leftovers afterward. Jesus says His disciples may have "more than twelve legions of angels" (Matt. 26:53). The woman had an issue of blood some twelve years before being healed (Mark 5:25–34). Jesus raised the twelve-year-old daughter of Jairus from the dead (see Mark 5:35–43).

If we diligently use the keys that the Lord has given us to interpret and apply the book of Revelation, it can truly become a book of personal revelation for us. As Jesus taught in the Book of Mormon: "And then shall my revelations which I have caused to be written by my servant John be unfolded in the eyes of all the people. Remember, when ye see these things, ye shall know that the time is at hand that they shall be made manifest in very deed" (Ether 4:16).

*About the Author*

ERIC RICHARDS GREW UP ATTENDING the Mountain View Baptist Church in San Diego before joining The Church of Jesus Christ of Latter-day Saints thanks to Elders Jolley and Hodson. His own mission began in Honduras and, following surgery to remove a bone tumor from his shin, ended in Alabama.

He met his wife at Especially For Youth, and after their marriage, he moved to Utah to teach seminary. He played water polo and volleyball for Utah State University, where he earned his MA in education.

Brother Richards has taught seminary and institute since 1996 and speaks at firesides all over the country each year. He is known for his constant smile, his popular *brotherichards* Instagram and Facebook accounts, and his upbeat CDs sold at Latter-day Saint bookstores nationwide. He is a beloved teacher at BYU Education Week and works as a session director for the EFY program.

Some random facts about Brother Richards: He's part Caucasian and part Polynesian, with a little Native American and African American thrown in. He's left-handed. He eats chocolate every day that he can. He can clap with one hand. He's an only child, his mom is an only child, and his grandmother was an only child; consequently, his family reunions are quite small.

Most of all, he loves teaching and being with valiant Latter-day Saints.